Mary Stott was born in Leicester in 1907, the daughter and grand-daughter of journalists. She began this career herself at the age of eighteen, working on various provincial newspapers including the *Manchester Evening News*, where she became its first woman sub-editor – a job she lost when though seniority should have offered her the job of 'copy-taster', she lost it because it had to go to a man. She was Woman's Page Editor of the *Guardian* from 1957–1971. In 1937 she married Kenneth Stott, who became Northern Editor of the *News Chronicle*, and has one daughter and two grand-daughters. Her widowhood – movingly described in this book – was a watershed in her life. She moved to London where she now lives and works. Always involved in the cause of women, she became an active member of the Women's Liberation Movement, and was a founder member of Women in Media. She has also been very active in all campaigns concerned with equal pay and anti-discrimination legislation.

She divides her time between her family, her writing, her passionate interest in music and her work for the Women's Movement.

VIRAGO is a feminist publishing imprint:

'It is only when women start to organize in large numbers that we become a political force, and begin to move towards the possibility of a truly democratic society in which every human being can be brave, responsible, thinking and diligent in the struggle to live at once freely and unselfishly'

Sheila Rowbotham, *Women, Resistance and Revolution*

FORGETTING'S NO EXCUSE

MARY STOTT

VIRAGO
QUARTET BOOKS LONDON

Published by VIRAGO 1975
an associated company of Quartet Books Limited
27 Goodge Street, London W1P 1FD

First published in Great Britain by
Faber and Faber Limited 1973

Copyright © 1973 by Mary Stott

ISBN 0 704 31801 6

Printed in Great Britain by litho by The Anchor Press Ltd
and bound by Wm Brendon & Son Ltd
both of Tiptree, Essex

For K. Stott's grand-daughters,
Caroline and *Charlotte*,
with love, gratitude and faith

FORGETTING'S NO EXCUSE

'This place smells of newsprint, said my daughter one day as she walked up the stairs of my Blackheath flat. 'As a matter of fact, so did the house at Heaton Moor.' I hadn't noticed, and that's not surprising, for I have lived with the smell of newspapers, the sharp smell of the ink, the warm smell of the paper, ever since I can remember. Ink in the veins, then, as well as in the nostrils? No, just ordinary Group A Rh.Neg blood.

When as a small child I told my dolls, 'I have some copy to write now,' I was only imitating my journalist parents, not indicating my destined future. That future was to be working in newspapers uninterruptedly for almost half a century, but it was also to be a human being with affections, passions and pursuits, and a child of my times. The strands of my life cannot be separated out; it is their interlocking, heredity and environment, work and home, that makes the pattern. Being a journalist's child made me a journalist; having a working mother made me expect to go on working myself; being born female hindered me from becoming the kind of newspaper journalist I would have liked to be; being a wife and mother probably made me a more effective women's page editor.

I have not been the kind of journalist who travels the world, covers wars, disasters and events of high political importance and who therefore may write books of reminiscence which are a contribution to history. Most of my life has been spent among the sort of unfamous but intelligent and concerned people who were my readers and who may read this book. They, I think, will understand my incredulity at having absorbed by some in-

1

explicable process of osmosis, from my work, my activities and surroundings, the attributes of a minor establishment figure. At having become the sort of person who is invited to present the prizes. (I hardly like to confess even now that it was my un-likely ambition as a schoolgirl to become respectworthy enough, important enough, to be a prize-presenter.) The sort of person to whom people say, 'Before I knew you I thought you were a very formidable lady.' The sort of person who is called, en-viously or disparagingly, 'a successful career woman', or who reads of herself with a wry giggle as 'a much respected doyenne of the women's page'. The sort of person who is actually *invited* to write a book.

Ah, but there is the difference between me and all the other people who understand how difficult it is to avoid sounding either coyly self-deprecating or pretentiously self-satisfied about having grown from an ugly duckling into a swan, even a small off-white swan in the backwater . . . the people who are aston-ished to have become O.B.E.s, dames, knights, life peers, lauded presidents of institutions and societies, heads of great schools. Like the old woman in the nursery rhyme, all of us say 'Can this be I?', but whereas most people can keep their amused surprise to themselves, or share it only with wife, husband or intimate friends, I am expected, indeed expect myself, to be able to write about it.

In fact being a newspaper woman has not only shaped the pattern of my life but shaped my habit of thought. The journalist develops antennae which cast about ceaselessly for stimuli. Whatever they sense is likely some day to be put into words on paper. Other people may forget, or ignore, but for a journalist, forgetting is no excuse. No excuse for having nothing of interest to say, nothing to write about; no excuse for not being able to relate what is happening now to what happened yesterday or the day before. Our minds train themselves to observe, note, analyse and carry in the memory whatever may be significant, in our own experience as well as other people's.

It is this habit of mind that dictates the shape of this book. It has driven me to try to dredge up, and sift for what was significant, my beginnings, my background, my conditioning, my way of life, and relate it to our times. What my journalist's antennae were responding to, especially in my *Guardian* days, was currents of social change, ground swells that grew into breakers crashing through the rocks of established attitudes . . . attitudes about women's role, marriage and family life, social behaviour and morality, public and private. So what my journalist's scribbling hand became restive to do was to get some

2

of it on paper . . . to verbalize the thoughts of a child of our times.

In 1975, four years after I began to write this book, it is still restive, for the pace of social change has increased remarkably, and even my own attitudes have been somewhat modified, demanding a few revisions for this paperback edition.

Even in my later sixties I still feel completely involved in my times, and more concerned to write about 'how it feels now', than 'how it was then'. Perhaps it is because my journalistic antennae are as much a part of me as my eyes or nose that I cannot retire from writing, or from activity. If so, how glad I am that my ancestry and my upbringing fixed a pattern that shaped my life.

1. NUCLEAR FAMILY WOMAN

Our childhood relationships explain a lot about what we become but I can never believe that they explain our basic nature. Brains, guts, physique, looks, temperament, we are born with, and even the ability to make the best of what we have got depends on native wit and will.

So . . . I was born with a good constitution, a goodish second-class mind, modest talents, and a lamentable lack of looks and guts. The good constitution has taken me into my sixties with never a bed-confining illness and I have never cracked under strain. The aptitudes, especially for words and music, which I inherited from all those gifted Bates and Waddingtons had a fertile soil in our family life. But those deficiencies – could they have been less of a handicap, or earlier cured, in any other family?

Before me there was Guy, fair, blue-eyed, even-tempered; a remarkably nice, easy child, I should imagine. Then Ralph William, who somehow mysteriously during our childhood became and remained 'John'. He was a desperately delicate baby and accident-prone child. Very beautiful, with his soulful grey eyes and golden curls like Bubbles. Obviously the sort of child to tug at the heart-strings of any mother, and the closest to ours temperamentally, I always thought. And then me. An accident, Guy's wife told me. A cross between a monkey and a heathen Chinee, my mother told me. I think she truly wanted a girl, but not a girl like me, pasty, lank-haired, charmless. She spent hours putting that boring hair into curling rags, quite uselessly. My feet were too big (once the shoe-repairer caused my brothers great mirth and me lasting shame by saying he had brought 'the young gent's' shoes).

5

From the age of eleven I had to wear glasses. How sad for my mother to have a graceless 'wizzly' daughter (her word for 'whiny'). How sad for me to follow two curly-haired brothers at a time when straight hair, now so fashionable, was thought to be a disaster for a girl. I was so thoroughly conditioned in childhood into thinking of myself as irrevocably plain that neither my daughter nor anyone else can nag or coax me out of the conviction that to try to make a silk purse out of this pig's ear would be a ludicrous and pitiful waste of time and money.

Writing this, I am not working off an old grudge against my mother. She was a child of her time, as we all are, and I never felt the necessity to 'forgive her – she gave me a great deal more than she took from me in self-confidence, and throughout my childhood she was the heart and core of my life. I went every-where with her, to meetings of the women Liberals, to fund-raising meetings for various charities, to 'comforts-making' parties during World War I. I have no recollection of ever being bored or restless. Children take for granted their parents' pattern of life. I took for granted that wherever Mother went, I went too. Until quite an advanced age I insisted on going to bed before she went out, to a meeting, a concert, a theatre, so that she could kiss me good-night. I remember one of our succession of dim little maids from the coal-mining villages of Leicestershire saying to me that there was only one person in the household she didn't like, and my refusing fiercely, passion-ately, to admit that that person could possibly be my mother.

Yet in early adolescence I had a violent revulsion against her. It was physical as well as emotional. I remember the unpleasant smell of her fingers (she smoked quite heavily in secret, and again it was a maid who let this out, and again I refused angrily at first to believe her). I remember shrinking away from the pressure of her body when we danced together at charity hops. I remember my horror at the idea of sharing a bed with her. The psychological revolt was probably all the more intense be-cause she had previously been the goddess figure. It was, I suppose, the revolt against being possessed, the blind yearning to protect my privacy, my separate identity. Mother would ask some kindly, harmless question about my friends, my school-mistresses, my interests, and I would stand rooted in suffocating silence. It was not that I would not speak but that I could not. Once when she asked me why, I managed to force out the words, 'I suppose I am afraid of you' and we were both drowned in helpless weeping. Poor Mother, what had she done to deserve it? As I feel no need to 'forgive' her, so I feel no need now to 'forgive' myself. She had had no chance of acquiring the psycho-logical insights that Freud, even Shaw, have given us. Neither of us knew that there is a basic element of hostility in the mother–daughter relationship. We know now, but still few of us can avoid exasperating or wounding a much-loved parent, a much-loved child. Will my granddaughters momentarily hate *their* mother, and if they do, will she understand?

Quite a lot of people, mostly men, tell me they can't remember anything about their childhood, but I am sure that writing any kind of autobiographical book forces one to think back to childhood. I was this and this and therefore I became . . . And when you dig back diligently it is the howling griefs, the terrors, the shames that are startlingly vivid. Worse than my consciousness of being a plain child was my awareness of being a coward, a fibber, a bad loser. We were a card-playing family and this was such a misery to me that I wonder how I bore it, even sulkily. I must have been about six when I crawled under the table because I was 'Old Maid'. There was a kind of whist we played in which the aim was to avoid winning a trick with Hearts. To be left with more Hearts than anyone else was a burning shame to me. No one likes a bad loser, so I think I was a most unlikeable child, but I swear it was less a desire to win, to excel, to be top dog that afflicted me than shame at being a failure, an unapproved person. Some children come into the world equable in nature and confident of being liked. They can't possibly know the misery of being timid. And come to that, they don't know, either, the incredulous relief of discovering that losing the game doesn't really matter. It would not be half so sweet pretending to my little granddaughters to cry piteously when I get the 'Old Maid' card, and being hugged and comforted by them, if I didn't remember the time when those sobs were painfully real. It wouldn't have been nearly so delightful to be told by my husband that I was comically incapable of telling an untruth if I hadn't remembered all those cowardly fibs. I can actually remember the occasion, in my early teens, when I was defeated at pingpong by my brother John and found I *didn't mind*.

It took much longer to conquer fear. The house I grew up in, 31 Highfield Street, Leicester, was large, four-storeyed, long-passaged, ill-lighted. When we went there, there was electric light only on the ground and first floors. Often we spent the evenings in the 'music room' on the first floor. To get to the kitchen at the back of the house I had to go down the stairs, along the passage, and through a pool of darkness by the side door. To get to my bedroom I had to get through another black patch at the turn of the stairs. To pass these spots needed a courage like going over the top into battle. I used to stand there rigid with terror. Terror of what? There were no words then, and there are no words now. It was not 'a bad man', 'a monster', 'a ghost' I feared. It was not even exclusively a fear of what might lurk in the dark, for the panic could strike even in daylight in that big old house if I was alone. It certainly was accentuated by what I read, but equally certainly was not caused by it. These terrors are atavistic and the worst of them is that children cannot talk about them, that they suffer them in secret.

It is impossible for parents to protect their children entirely against these fears, though one can help if they become evident, but any parent who tells me that children *enjoy* the *frisson* of horror stories makes my blood run cold. A few may, but for others, terror can blight years of their life. Even in my Co-op days, when I was well into my twenties, I was almost paralysed with panic walking at night from some small country station to a conference centre, between a long avenue of great black trees. I was so ashamed to be so frightened that I never spoke of it. To be fearless now, to be able to identify the creaks of furniture, the draughts that swing doors, the thumps that are a neighbour going upstairs to bed, is still a relief to be consciously savoured. It happened, remarkably, when World War II faced us with identifiable fears in the shape of bombs and gas. The fear of the unreal faded away, and even in Washington or New York I feel no terror of burglars, muggers, rapists.

So there is the worst of my childhood, written down to explain my inadequacies. Almost everyone's childhood leaves scars. I was very touched to meet a contemporary, not only a contented wife, mother and grandmother, but a successful writer of fiction, who said to me, 'All through my childhood I heard my brothers say, "Oh we don't want *you*".' But that doesn't mean that either for her or for me it was all misery. My brothers, though kinder, kept me firmly in my place and deflated my childish and adolescent enthusiasms, but the fun we shared far outweighed the rough side of family life. We were a family of gigglers, especially my mother. It was a Bates characteristic. I remember Uncle Frank, weeping with laughter, because he had suddenly imagined visually the old joke 'a-bun-dance on the table'. I remember Mother, who had offered sixpence to the person who made her laugh most during Christmas, clutching the bannisters at the foot of the stairs and gasping, 'You can all give up. Daddy's won the sixpence. He's put his cardigan on upside down.' I remember a game we used to play with the uncles, a sort of snap, in which the two people who drew the same card had to stare at one another until one gave way and laughed. I hope families still laugh like that, helpless, aching, speechless, weeping. Alas and alas it is a long while since I did.

The overt joys, in fact, did outweigh the secret miseries which now have insisted on being revealed. The deficiencies have all been compensated for, the scars healed over; the roots have never withered. I am very thankful to have grown up in a nuclear family, a family so strongly attached and so mutually supportive. We were exceptionally lucky, of course, in that the Bates family was large, talented and gay, and that my mother, the oldest, never let any of them slip out of her ken, not even Charlie who went as a boy to America. I was lucky in that Guy and John both married women who became my dear friends; that when Johnny died of tuberculosis in his early forties we did not 'lose' Ella or her three boys; that when Guy and I both lost our partners we were able to draw easily and naturally closer together; that our family did not devour, but gave sustenance, and still does.

The nuclear family is under constant attack; worse, it is in danger because it is so shrunken. There are fewer siblings to teach one another the elements of fair play, and that the world does not revolve round one's own tiny ego. Children have less chance to learn to accept knocks and jeers, to stand together as allies against the adult world. Must we not think of an alternative supportive framework? Isn't this the very best argument for nursery schools and co-education, to keep children in groups throughout their growing-up years, to provide them with siblings? We may, I hope, find that the children of divorced parents have a bond with step-brothers and -sisters and that step-parents who are civilized in their attitudes can replace the galaxy of uncles and aunts we had.

One needs permanent relationships. One needs friends. I think we should hear less of men and women who are looking in adult life for a mother figure or a father figure if we were more aware of the need for friends. In my miserable adolescence, trying to escape the domination of my mother (I never did, because she died when I was twenty-three, before we had learned to accept one another as two like-minded adults) I moved into the orbit of my father, hitherto a rather shadowy figure, and learned to love very dearly this quiet man, so well-informed, so undemanding and affectionate, but my need was for the reassurance of affection and approval from a contemporary. Having come to think of myself as unlovable and being quite unready for relationships with the other sex, I blossomed remarkably in the friendship, in the sixth form, of Connie Barton, now Bond. It happened because there were only the two of us doing Classics. I thought her most of the things I was not – beautiful in a serene kind of way, with blue-grey eyes and pretty hair. Tidy, well-adjusted, an approved kind of person,

9

unlike scruffy me. We walked home from school hand in hand and stood hours on street corners talking. We sat close together in an armchair, occasionally kissed and hugged. The idea of any further physical exploration simply never occurred to us. 'Lesbian' meant a person living on Lesbos, perhaps a poet, like Sappho. No doubt our parents (and my brothers) thought we were embarrassingly mawkish, but if they were worried they never said so. Perhaps in this they were luckier than today's parents, who know so much more about homosexuality. It was accepted that girls always had crushes, on schoolmistresses or on one another. It was just one more tiresome phase of adolescence and we should grow out of it. If anyone had put it into my mind that my love for my friend was 'unnatural' and 'perverted' I think I should have gone out of my mind with shame and horror. I know now that there is nothing unnatural or perverted in affection between people of the same sex and that in adolescence it occurs between many who are basically heterosexual and in them is a valuable preparation for adult love. I wish that young people, especially girls, could be encouraged to enjoy single sex friendships rather than being pressurised during puberty by romantic fiction and advertising into full sexual relationships for which they are too immature, and which may result in schoolgirl pregnancies and abortions. And if in the course of single-sex friendships some young people discover that they are undeniably homosexual, isn't it better that they should accept this, rather than being terrified of being 'perverted', or rushing into marriage in a hopeless, and usually disastrous, attempt to escape from their basic nature? There are probably many more true homosexuals in our community than most of us guess, and I hope the day will come when sexual orientation is not a matter of 'right' and 'wrong'. But I am equally concerned that the friendship of women, from schooldays onwards, should be given its full value. Why does it sound 'soppy' to talk gratefully of one's women friends? I can say on a platform at a prize-giving, 'You'll forget the names of half the boys you go out with, but if you leave school with a couple of real friends they will be a strength to you all your life', but words stick in my gullet when I try to express what my women friends mean to me – my contemporaries at school, Connie Barton, who married a Baptist minister; Emily Frisby, distinguished meteorologist; Helen Fletcher, who became my friend in the darkest time of my life; Nesta Roberts, my *Guardian* colleague, and many others, whose friendship has been a source of stimulus, comfort and fun, all my life.

My friendship with Connie was in embryo the pair bond that I think the best guarantee of human happiness. She became engaged to her divinity student while she was at Newnham. I took much longer to cope with relationships with men, but through all those unhappy years of being rejected, of trying to prop up a man whom my idealistic self-sacrifice could never have salvaged, I was unconsciously looking for a man friend of the quality of Connie Bond. I was twenty-eight when I found one. K Stott and I were friends for thirty years.

In marriage I was liberated. I know that saying this divides me from some of my young Women's Liberation friends, but it is the exact truth. I was liberated from the fear of inadequacy. What made me able to cope with disasters at work, what made me grow in courage, fortitude, even in independence, was that K Stott loved me, admired me, was strong for me – and also depended on me. He thought I was the head of the house. I thought he was. I do not like to think what might have become of me if we had not met and married. 'Liberation' is having the opportunity to 'do your own thing'. Marriage enabled me to do it much more confidently, more successfully. Women who declare as an article of faith that women can never be 'free' within the institution of marriage seldom know, literally, what they are talking about. None of them, so far as I can discover, has had the opportunity to find out how after ten, twenty, thirty years the marriage bond can become not a constricting ligature, but the rope on which climbers depend for each other's safety. With this rope you *can* securely climb. Sidney Webb once said '1 and 1 make 2. But if you bring 1 and 1 close together they make 11'. So it was with us.

But we started, in 1937, from a point that many young people still have not arrived at. I had been financially independent since I was about twenty-one; I was an established journalist in Manchester, quite well known because of my activity in the National Union of Journalists. I was four years older than K – in fact earning ten shillings a week more than he did – and he was only at the beginning of his career on the *News Chronicle*. If K had had the conventional idea of marriage he would not have looked twice at me. Perhaps he wouldn't have looked twice if he had only met the vice-chairman of the N.U.J. branch, but we met when he came to live in the same house – I in my first flat, on the ground floor, he with two men friends on the top floor. So he knew, as we came easily and quite quickly into love and understanding, what kind of a person I was, and I knew that I didn't have to sound his views on marriage or to fear that he would ever resent my job or wish to curb my freedom.

11

After my three or four very rough years, I was incredulously happy at 400 The Cliff, Salford, up and down the stairs between my flat and the boys'. When dear little Mrs Evans, our tiny Welsh 'treasure', was not looking after them I was. I had a letter on my retirement from one of them, W. P. Hamsher ('Hammy' to us), head of the *Daily Express*'s Paris bureau, recalling an N.U.J. meeting: 'You sent a message to me across the floor of the house, entrusting it to Jack Yeadon. The chairman's compliments to Mr Hamsher, and if you don't stop interrupting you won't get a hot-water bottle in your bed tonight.' I was wrapped in love, comradeship and laughter, confident for the first time in my life that everything was going to be all right. (That didn't actually prevent last-minute 'bride's panic', but it lasted only until we had signed the register. From then on I had no moment of doubt.)

So we got married, not exactly conventionally. My parents being both dead we had to make our own arrangements. I moved across the road a day or two before to the fine, decrepit early-Victorian house we were renting, I think for ten shillings a week, and after the register office ceremony we entertained our friends and relations there. We set off for a weekend honeymoon in Wales in an aged car borrowed from Tom Baistow, then *News Chronicle*, now *New Statesman*, giving a couple of friends a lift on their way. The car broke down in Chester and K spent the first morning of our married life tinkering with it in the rain. But the real unconventionality was that I had a thin platinum ring for an engagement ring and was married with it, and insisted, only half in fun, on giving K half the wedding licence fee, saying, 'You are not buying me for 7s. 6d.' I was an equal earner, equally responsible for the home. It would have seemed shaming to me to be financially dependent on my husband or any other human being. But if I was going to work outside the home it seemed to me that I must replace the wife's traditional services there, so I always paid the wages of all the domestic help we had and for the food and cleaning materials, while K paid the rent or mortgage, the rates, for the fuel and later the car. 'Improvements' we shared. I cannot remember any disagreement about money in the whole of our married life. K was the spender, I the saver. I loved his generosity, he was grateful for my ability to hang on to money and would pay steadily into my account if we were saving for some special purpose. 'My little pile' we called it. 'Mummy is our mobile bank,' said our daughter as a little girl at Southport flower show. There are many different ways of managing a married couple's finances which will work well if there is mutual trust and respect, but if I were starting off again now I would think that three accounts were better than either one or two – his, mine, and ours. I feel the same about sharing the work of the home. It should be on the same equal partnership basis, each contributing what he or she is best equipped to do. So you get a sharing of responsibility and some freedom of personal choice.

It would be dishonest to imply that K and I never irritated, displeased or hurt one another. But it is true that we never felt bored or constricted by our marriage, and that there never was a patch so bad that either of us feared, even for half a day, that it might break down. Many people, I suppose, would think it an odd kind of set up, for during most of our thirty years together he worked by night and I worked by day. People misguidedly pitied me. I suppose they must have pitied K for having a working wife. They didn't need to. We thought we were lucky not to be under one another's feet all the time. He could 'cool off' after a hard night's work, at the Press Club, knowing that when he got home I should be in bed and probably asleep. (Though in fact I always woke and worried if he was much past his usual time.) I could enjoy my music, my friends, without feeling I was neglecting him – though in fact we liked one another's friends. Men always say to me that 'he was a man's man'. Perhaps I am 'a woman's woman', but K liked the intelligent, mature women of whom I was fond, and I liked talking newspaper gossip with his friends.

I can understand why younger women rebel against the 'marriage bond'. They want to be solely responsible for their own lives. They see all around them the wretched plight, when marriage breaks up, of women who have been economically dependent. They see couples who, apparently, stick together out of habit, or through economic and social pressures, when all joy has gone. They can control their own fertility so that they can safely move from lover to lover without the risk of bringing into the world a child who might force them into a permanent relationship. It is true that most normal people have it in them to love more than one person very truly, and that falling in love is a glorious thing. They ask me and, I have to admit understandably, 'Why sacrifice this freedom for some questionable security in old age?' To explain why is almost as difficult as to explain to a blind man the colour of a rose. It involves trying to explain tenderness and the gradual integration of two personalities so that each draws from and gives to the other what he or she needs. Halving trouble, doubling joy – how absurdly trite it sounds. But now I am alone I know that like most truisms it is *true*, and that you cannot learn its truth in a relationship lasting only five months, or even five years.

The young jeer at a middle-aged couple sitting in a café

13

having apparently nothing to say. Perhaps they are indeed completely bored with one another. But perhaps one knows the other is sad, troubled, or just plain tired, and is waiting, in loving-kindness, for the moment when it is right to speak. One knows these things about the man or woman with whom one has shared bed, bedroom, kitchen, work, play, friends, griefs. Can you truly comfort any human being however much you long to, unless you are, as it were, part of him or her? Only saints can be as totally involved as that with more than one person. And perhaps that middle-aged couple will comfort one another in bed, though he is paunchy, bald, thick-necked, red-veined, and she is scraggy, grey, lined, round-shouldered. Would *you* fancy going to bed with him or her? More importantly, if you looked like that, would anyone fancy going to bed with *you*? The chances are that the person within that unappetizing body is so dear to the other, that the ungainly shape is actually *loved*, warts and all.

In this unfair society in which we live, continuity of love is more important for women than for men. Though some women can and do preserve their looks by great expenditure of time and money, it is scarcely one in a thousand who, from middle-age on, can inspire desire in a desirable lover. The Personal advertisements are full of widowers and divorcés looking for a 'warm, slim, attractive female', usually up to 20 years younger, for 'a meaningful relationship'. It makes me squirm a bit to think that their postbags are probably full of letters from lonely widows, deserted wives and single women anxious to change 'Miss' to 'Mrs'. But even apart from these sad lonely hearts, it is still true that a man with money and some distinction can woo an attractive girl half his age. His admiration may flatter her. She may be very willing to marry him. The admiration of an older woman would make most attractive young men shudder with distaste. It may not always be so, if the balance of the sexes changes, as it shows signs of doing, and it becomes harder for a man to find a mate of his own age, or younger, but even for women who are now quite young, there will be few men to find them physically desirable when they are in their fifties, let alone their sixties. Do they think, perhaps, that all passion will be spent? It seldom is, and is less likely to fade for people to whom it has been very important. I have been told fiercely that the young cannot live by the rule of laying up emotional, sexual, security for their old age, any more than by skimping themselves to put money in the bank. Perhaps not. I can say no more than that the joy of having a mate who finds your body as desirable as when you married is very great, and that it is not only very lonely, but very humiliating to know that never again will any man you fancy, fancy you. It needs a lot of inner strength to cope with that situation. Perhaps lifelong independence will give such strength. So does having been one half of a pair bond.

No child was more longed for than Catherine Lindsay Stott. When I married, at twenty-nine, my arms were already feeling empty and I was apt to feel weepy at the sight of a woman with a child in a pram, so that I can never mock or deplore 'broodiness' even in a woman who already has a family. In many women the desire for children is a very strong, deep emotion, not at all easy to cope with for women who have miscarriage after miscarriage, are infertile, or are intellectually convinced that two children is their 'share'. I was thirty-five when Catherine was born and all my sympathy rushes out to the women whose desire for children is frustrated, in these times when all the talk is of fertility *control*. The baby decided to make her appearance at a very inconvenient time. K was already in the Navy and I was living alone in a flat. Plans were laid for us to move round the corner to a house in which K's parents and sister would join me to help care for the child, but I felt an overpowering longing to be with my own people for the birth, so parked myself for six weeks before the birth and six weeks after with my sisters-in-law in Leicestershire.

I always wanted a daughter. So, happily, did K. The first baby I knew was Kitty Staines, next door in Leicester, whose sisters used to summon me to sing lullabies if she would not settle. Then there was my niece Anne, the most beautiful baby I ever saw. Then Elizabeth and Mary Dennis, enchanting daughters of my friend Helen, whom K came to love as much as I did. Like Barrie, we thought, 'Daughters are the thing'. So when I came out of the anaesthetic to hear the nurse saying, 'You've got a beautiful daughter, Mrs Stott,' I murmured, 'Have I? How lovely.' So much for the myth that all mothers want to bear strong sons. This was in 1943. K had just finished his commission training in the Navy. He came home on leave the night the baby was born, a fortnight later took us back to my brother's home, and that night left for a destination unknown – in fact the Mediterranean, to serve on a mine-sweeping corvette and, later, to take part in the landings at Anzio and Salerno. It was more than two years before we saw him again. Poor K. Poor Catherine. Poor me. How many people remember now that there were thousands of us in this situation? Wives who had to sweat it out without sex or companionship or, often, enough money; children to whom 'Daddy' was a word, not a person. And always living in fear. Night after night I used to hear over the radio, 'The minesweepers went in first'; and it

15

could have been K and sometimes it *was* K, whose ship was at risk and who might never have come back.

I know that we were luckier than most. I could earn enough to maintain the family, we had a settled home and my in-laws were wonderfully kind and supportive. I owe them a debt of gratitude beyond what I can repay. But it was not only because my husband was very far away and in constant danger that those were the two most difficult years of my life. The ways of the Bates and the Waddingtons were not the ways of the Stotts. I can well believe that I was a greater strain on their patience than they were on mine. We did not laugh at the same things, we did not have the same attitudes. Granny Stott was a noble woman, but it was hard on me that though I maintained the home she was mistress of it. For fear of her disapproval I paced the room at night with a howling child in my arms until the clock said it was time to feed her. I raced home from work at lunch time to breast-feed the baby, after which she was put down for a long sleep, so that when I raced home again in the evening she was too lively to want to go to sleep and I dare not leave her, as I would if I had been on my own, to cry it out.

Well, at least I learned two lessons – that a child needs the involvement of its father as well as its mother from the beginning (my daughter's relations with her father were never easy) and that grandmothers must keep their traps shut. They may believe, as I do, that breast-feeding is not only best but an incomparable pleasure to the mother if all goes well, but no mother should be pressured into a decision, least of all by her mother or mother-in-law. Fashions in child care change. I feel rather bitter about having been conditioned by the Truby King clock-watching regime. A friend of mine actually reared her child by the Truby King dictum that it was somehow bad for a baby to be too much cuddled and kissed. Oh for heaven's sake, how can a baby know it is loved except by cuddling and hugging? Thank goodness I knew that such austerity was so alien to my nature as to be impossible for me. But whatever the currently accepted regime for child care, it is granny's job to dote, not to dictate.

When my daughter told me she was pregnant my first thought was, 'Oh goodness, she's too young'; the second was a sense of satisfaction that there would be another child to carry on the line, to inherit whatever gifts had passed through my line, my husband's, the father's. I felt this so strongly that it made me wonder how any parents could reject their daughter's child, even if that child is illegitimate, of mixed race, or handicapped.

It would still be their grandchild, blood of their blood. My daughter's child was *our* child, not just her child, their child. Still is. Naturally I wanted to be with my daughter for her first child's birth. I told her I would do whatever I could for her home-coming in running the household, washing the nappies, heating the bottles. But in the years of her growing up I hadn't been much of a baby-handler and I told her, 'I think I've forgotten all I knew about coping with a newborn infant. You cope with the baby. I'll cope with the house.' So I was totally unprepared for the extraordinary emotion I felt when Caroline was put in my arms. This little soft thing with its wobbly head tucked against my shoulder gave me such an all-pervading sense of physical joy that I have never since quite believed that the orgasm was necessarily the highest human physical satisfaction. A baby again in the arms that had been used for everything else for twenty years or more. *Our* baby. I suspect that the grandmother savours the new baby more consciously, more gratefully, than the mother herself, because her joy is not overshadowed with anxiety. So, at least, it was with me.

And with a great many other women. In October 1971 I was sitting at breakfast, on the opening day of an international conference of women journalists in Washington, with Marjorie Proops, of the *Daily Mirror*, Anne Blythe Munro, a leading women's magazine journalist, and Winifred Crum Ewing, administrator of the Women's Press Club of London. And what were these four high-powered journalists doing? Showing around snapshots of their grandchildren. Grandmothers nowadays are a sisterhood. I doubt if it was so in our grandmothers' time. They had had so many babies of their own that their children's babies were not very remarkable to them. But they are to us, because we only had one, or two, or three, and it was so long ago. I remember a woman in the *Guardian* canteen in Manchester whose son had a son about the time my daughter had a daughter. Despite her yellow curls and pink make-up she always looked tired and depressed. But when there was a baby in the house again, she shone. So, I am sure, did I. Men colleagues teased me, a little mischievously perhaps, about being a granny, imagining that it must have made me feel old and resentful. Little they knew. A baby is a better rejuvenator for an ageing woman than a face-lift, monkey glands or whatever now is the fashionable way of trying to recapture lost youth. I can still play 'Ring-a-ring-a-roses', fall down and kick my legs in the air and I am very sure that nothing else but the wish to please our little girls would make me so skittish. When younger mothers confide their worries to me about their teenage children I smile and say, 'Just wait . . . just wait . . . bringing up your

17

own children is all worth while. One day you will have grand-children.'

Almost every widow I have ever talked with has said the same thing, 'It isn't sex I miss; it is someone to touch.' Touching, in our society, is not an adult thing to do, which is obviously why we love our dogs and cats so dearly. Thank heaven for little children who have not learned that it is not done to 'cuddle and kiss'. They climb on your knee; they hold your hand as you walk along; they say, 'I love you, Granny'; when you ring the doorbell they tumble over one another rushing to open it, 'Granny! Granny!' And they provide what you may well be short of, a reason to go on living. Could Caroline, who seems to understand so well how things work and are put to-gether, become an architect or an engineer? Could Charlotte, who listened intently to Mozart at eighteen months and sang 'Frère Jacques' in tune when she was barely two, become a musician? How can one bear not to wait around to find out?

I would not exchange these little girls, K Stott's grand-daughters, for a string of lovers, nor for freedom to 'live my own life', nor to escape the constriction of family ties. I have had many talks with liberated young women who intend to remain childless. I do not think them 'selfish' or 'unnatural' as many people used to, and some still do. I respect them, know that many lead useful and unselfish lives, and sympathize with their desire to build up a network of lasting relationships which will be as secure as blood ties. I hope they will succeed – but I wonder if in their sixties they will have the strong comfort and joy, the powerful sense of the continuity of life, that my grand-daughters give me.

2. SITTING ON A FENCE

I began life as a little Liberal; I think I shall end it as some kind of a liberal. A long journey, painfully dis-carding Free Trade and *laissez-faire* in my late teens; turning leftwards but resisting the fashionable drama and glamour of Communism in my early twenties; deprived of faith in the

18

perfectibility of man by improvements in his way of life in my thirties; learning blow by blow in my forties and fifties that Socialism had become a label for a political party rather than for an ideal or a crusade; confronted in my sixties with the fact that 'liberal' has become a word of abuse for thousands upon thousands of young people as passionately moved by the injustice of our society as I was in the 1920s and '30s. There isn't really any label now to cover my kind of beliefs – social justice, government by consent, international brotherhood and non-violence.

We were a very political family. The first memory I can date accurately is riding around in a car with a green ribbon round my hat. It must have been the General Election of 1911. The people next door were Conservative and their daughter, a little older than I, bragged to me over the garden wall that the Conservative colour, blue, was much prettier than green. Privately I agreed, but stuck loyally to my guns. 'Yes, but yellow is the Liberal colour too, and that's just as nice as green.' Probably about the same time there was some Happening in Leicester – a bazaar, perhaps – in the old Temperance Hall, at which I was required to hand a bouquet to the visiting celebrity. (My dim memory is that she was a Lady Crewe.) They told me which she was, how to hand over the flowers and curtsy, but no one had told me what to do next. I stood bewildered in the middle of that vast platform and then, on the far side, saw Nunkie, dear reassuring Nunkie. I took to my heels, ran and leapt into his arms. It must have been a wow.

'Nunkie' was T. W. Smith, the Liberal Party agent in Leicester who came to lodge with us during the election as agent for Sir Gordon Hewart, later Lord Hewart, Lord Chief Justice, and stayed something like a dozen years, my mother's devoted friend and mine, even closer than any of the real uncles, charmers as they were, and a source of political anecdotes until he died in his mid-eighties.

As soon as we were old enough we were allowed to stay up for the declaration of the polls – very much more exciting then than now when the psephologists can predict the result to television viewers from the first handful of marginal constituencies. By my teens I was helping to deliver election literature. I heard David Lloyd George speak, and, of course, Winston Churchill, who became Liberal candidate for West Leicester. My mother got his signature for my autograph book – but he was a great disappointment to me. I was in the Liberal Club the night the poll was declared and he was defeated. Even when he was wartime premier and his splendid command of the oratorical art moved me to the guts, I never forgot his face that

19

night. Sullen. Sulky. A bad loser. Churchill returned, of course, to the Conservative party soon after his Leicester defeat.

My father was a Liberal of the old school. The one political subject that would get him on to an election platform was Free Trade, about which he could talk in an academic kind of way, unflustered but uninspiring, until the candidate arrived. My mother was much more concerned with social progress and it was she who had the gift of platform presence. Yet it was my father who understood better my intellectual doubts when, having joined the *Leicester Mail* I came into contact with what we now call 'the Lefties' – members of the Independent Labour Party Guild of Youth – and a Communist or two. During the 1929 General Election I suggested putting up a poster for the Labour candidate in my bedroom window. My mother was appalled; my father smiled. 'I don't think much of any young person who doesn't start by being a rebel' was his attitude. The poster did not go up but I voted Labour and always have. My tiny niche in history is that in that election I was a 'flapper voter' – one of the first batch of women entitled to vote at twenty-one on the same terms as men. I went to the polling station in a scarlet frock, a little disappointed that putting a cross on a bit of paper was so undramatic. In the Conservative-owned *Leicester Mail* that night there was uncontrollable glee, when Labour was returned with a small but viable majority.

This break from the traditional family political allegiance meant a genuine intellectual struggle for me. Adults are too apt to think that the young cannot work out political attitudes for themselves and are simply caught up by whatever is trendy and 'in'. 'Lefty' politics *were* very much 'in' during the late twenties and early thirties but it was a sizeable struggle to shake off the ideas I had accepted from my parents as being natural and right and I don't doubt that intelligent, idealistic young people have a similar mental effort to make today. It was not only my *Mail* colleagues, like Mike Flannagan who came to us from the old *Sunday Worker* with his wife Elizabeth, daughter of the veteran Communist Tom Mann, who jolted my thinking, but my contacts with the Conservative ladies, whose meetings and social gatherings I had to cover for the paper. They shocked me. Sometimes they still do. Their attitude then tended to be, 'It's no use giving the working classes council houses: they will keep coal in the bath and gradually turn them into slums. They don't know any better.' And the comparable attitude now? 'Of course they're so mad about Bingo they leave their children alone in the house night after night.' Them, the lower orders, and Us, the upholders of Values. Them, greedy for wage increases, and Us, finding it difficult to maintain our children at public schools. Them, up to all sorts of dodges to get undeserved Social Security and Us employing accountants to find ways to get round income tax. It is quite unfair to say that Right is divided from Left by generosity of spirit but it has always seemed to me that it is one aspect of the quite genuine division of political approach. Right seeks to maintain the *status quo* fearing that any change will be for the worse. Left wants change hoping it will be for the better. I have not turned out to be a political animal like my forebears, because I am temperamentally a fence-sitter, but in those times of political crisis when the political division is clear, I have always found myself on the side of the underprivileged, the have-nots. I can, with difficulty, bear the inertia and complacency of the Right, but cannot endure the Right's assumption of superiority, the habit of mind that justifies *despising* the underprivileged.

In my later days in Leicester involving myself in Left politics was exhilarating but, as for so many students today, pretty superficial. We sang the Red Flag and The Internationale at I.L.P. gatherings. We joined in the adulation of Jimmie Maxton and the new stars, Oswald and Cynthia Mosley. We thought Margaret Bondfield, the first woman Cabinet Minister, rather a drab little mouse. It took the journey north to Bolton in 1931 to open my eyes to what 'the Slump', the great Depression really meant – jobless men hanging about street corners in the deathly quiet of this Lancashire mill town after the bustling brightness of Leicester, which remained one of the most prosperous cities of Europe. I still lived in a mainly middle-class environment and the organizations whose works I admired and tried to foster, like the Women Citizens Association, were all middle class. But in Bolton I learned about the Means Test; about the 'minimum diet' worked out by Ministry of Health doctors who decided that 5s. 10d. was enough for a single person to maintain health; I learned about the women who never went to the doctor despite prolapses and cancer fears, who bought spectacles at Woolworths and never had their bad teeth attended to because they couldn't afford it. Those were the days of 'Love on the Dole' and the hunger marches.

When I moved to the Co-operative Press in Manchester in 1933 I learned a lot more about the economic facts of life. A conference in West Hartlepool shook me rigid. Hardly any shops were open in the main street, because no one had any money to spend. The 'chambermaid' in the hotel where we stayed was a young man – the only work he could get. For the first time I had to think of myself, with some bewilderment and embarrassment, as 'middle class' because my parents had never worked with their hands and I had had a grammar school education. But the ideology of the co-operative movement suited me like a glove – an idealistic basis but a practical strategy. It was not idealistic Robert Owen with his communes who got the co-operative movement off the ground, but twenty-eight poor weavers of Rochdale with their beautifully simple device of paying dividend on purchases rather than dividend on capital. The perfect launching pad, it seemed, for workers' ownership and control; no need for capital or capitalists. The profitable act of shopping at your own shop would provide a surplus sufficient to build up funds to finance wholesale agencies and later factories which would sell only to co-operative societies and so all still be in the hands of co-operative members on a basis of one man (or one woman) one vote. From the simple store in Toad Lane, Rochdale, sprang the mighty Co-operative Wholesale Society, the Scottish Co-operative Wholesale Society and consumer co-operative movements all round the world, notably in Scandinavia. The co-operative idea still seems to be the best alternative, combining idealism and commonsense, to the profit motive. But the dividend is no longer the attraction it was. In my youth poor families drew the 'divi' on quarter day to buy shoes for the children and other necessities for the children. My beautiful Grotrian Steinway piano was bought by my mother largely out of accumulated 'divi' in the Co-op. Many, if not most, retail co-operative societies now give trading stamps rather than 'divi' on purchases. The idea of 'saving up' is less compulsive. There is social security, including supplementary benefit, and full employment – and there is inflation, which tends to make nonsense of thrift.

Why, in the climate of the Welfare State, which would seem propitious for the advance of the co-operative movement, has it flagged and so far slipped back? In economic terms the enormous growth of supermarket chains and international manufacturing cartels is no doubt the explanation. In the human terms in which I saw it in my own Co-op days, I think a fatal flaw was the refusal to abandon its working-class exclusivity. Even before the 1948 Education Act opened up higher education to many more working-class children, the sons and daughters of co-operative members had won scholarships to grammar schools and to universities. But they were not recruited into the service of the movement – it took its recruits almost exclusively from people who had left school at fourteen, both staff and members of retail societies' management boards and the directors of the C.W.S. and other central organizations; and these men (they were almost entirely men) had little training in either economics or politics – nor were the store buyers sensitive to the fact that 'working-class' tastes were drawing much nearer to those of the so-called middle class. Because – it seemed to me, product of a middle-class grammar school background – there was no room for the graduate in the co-operative leadership, it had, by my time, fallen into the hands of men of only second-class calibre. The Labour Party has always drawn strength from middle-class intellectuals, and Ernest Bevin did not find it impossible to work alongside Clement Attlee – each, in fact, had respect and affection for the other. Why did not this happen in the co-operative movement? Why was there suspicion on the one side and lack of interest on the other?

The working-class exclusivity bothered me all the time I was working for the Co-operative Press and bothers me still, but I loved and venerated the women of the co-operative movement, whose courage, persistence and loyalty seemed to me often heroic, for though most of them were under-educated and many were scarcely above the poverty line, they learned to speak in public, go on deputations, organize and preside at great conferences. To me the most remarkable thing about the Women's Co-operative Guild was the training it gave in the art of government, its completely democratic structure. It was not possible for any woman with more leisure, more money, more personality, more of the art of the demagogue, more status, to shoot up into leadership. Every candidate for office had to serve her term at the lower committee levels, branch, district and region, before she could stand for office on the central executive body, and during these probationary years she would attend one-day or weekend schools on administration or special subjects in the co-operative programme. This framework was worked out by two shining examples of that extraordinary genus, the English spinster – Margaret Llewelyn Davies (whose aunt, Emily Davies, was the true begetter of Girton) and her lifelong friend Lilian Harris. Miss Harris was the organizer, and Miss Llewelyn Davies the inspiration of shy, under-privileged women whose confidence in their ability to speak in public, to take part in deputations, to Parliament and to the mighty C.W.S., she was able to build up by the gentle strength of a personality of rare beauty. I think these brave co-operative women of the thirties faced hazards not unlike those that face the brave women of the seventies. They were courted by the middle-class 'Establishment' for their special 'working-class' contribution and they firmly resisted being seduced by what they saw as the flattery of the enemies of their class. The *avant-garde* women today are courted by the mass media in aid of lively 'copy' and TV and radio confrontations, and have learned, often painfully, that the sharp interviewing techniques, the snide reporting of some journalists make publicity not an asset but a threat, and are destructive of their own and their movement's credibility. In a way it was easier for the co-operative women to stand their ground, but I am sure that this was partly because they were so thoroughly trained. Women's Liberation groups are rightly distrustful of masculine methods of leadership, of hierarchical structures and of demagogues. They are trying to work out something different and better, but I hope they will have the patience, the modesty and the persistence of the co-operative women to achieve their aims.

It seemed to some of us in the thirties that the rigidity of the co-operative training system placed a premium on mediocrity and provided no way of keeping in the public eye, as leaders and spokesmen, the able women it had brought forward (far too few were elected to the major co-operative bodies) once their term of national office was completed, but it did produce a remarkable number of women who could run a meeting, even a national conference, with scarcely flustered efficiency. One or two chairmen of standing orders – a job needing a cool head and a platform presence, if ever there was one – stay in my mind as models.

Nowadays 'reformers' are out of fashion, and admiration is given only to 'activists', to the people who want to change things NOW. But I believe politics is the art of the possible and that to impose radical change against the climate of opinion inevitably produces a violent anti-reaction. My own greatest admiration is for the people who go on patiently and steadfastly pushing change along, who do not allow disappointment to deflect them, who never give up. The co-operative women were like this. I had another great bond with them, their pacifism. Margaret Llewelyn Davies set them on this road, and her successor, as general secretary of the Women's Co-operative Guild, Eleanor Barton, who had come up from the ranks and was both a notable orator and a notable activist. It was she, I think, who conceived the idea of wearing a white poppy, instead of the red, on Armistice Day. In many ways it was easier to be a pacifist in the 1930s than now – no one had forgotten the vast, senseless slaughter of our young men in World War I – yet it took as much courage, I think, to wear the white poppy on 11th November as it did for the Committee of 100 to lie down in the road in the 1960s.

You could say that in the 1920s and 1930s international solidarity, especially with Russia, was fashionable among the workers and pacifism among the intellectuals. Faith in the ability of the League of Nations to prevent war lasted much

longer than faith in the United Nations. What we debated endlessly was whether an international police force and military
sanctions were consonant with our view of non-violence. We
rejoiced when the Oxford Union voted against 'fighting for
King and Country'; we took part in the League of Nations
Peace Ballot; we signed Dick Sheppard's Peace Pledge. Some
of us enrolled in his Peace Army, committed to interposing
itself between opposing military forces (including a friend of
mine who when war broke out almost immediately enlisted in
the WRNS!). The Japanese invasion of China should have
warned us that the League of Nations was far too weak to stop
war – but the Far East seemed much more remote then, before
the coming of television. What broke the strength of the pacifist
will to peace was not despair about the failures of the League of
Nations, much less a resurgence of patriotic fervour. It was the
rise of Fascism. It hit us hard in the co-operative movement.
Many co-operative leaders were imprisoned, including Emmy
Freundlich, president of the International Co-operative Guild
and Food Minister of the Austrian Government. There was
Mussolini's rape of Abyssinia; there was the traumatic Spanish
Civil War, which divided Right from Left, Red from Black,
more sharply than perhaps anything in my lifetime and for
many idealistic young people destroyed for ever the faith in non-
violence which Gandhi's success in India had seemed to make a
viable method of rebellion.

In 1938 K and I had planned to go to Vienna, but as it had
by then fallen to the Nazis we decided on a package 'train
cruise' round Italy. We arrived in Rome just before Hitler
arrived to visit Mussolini and watched their triumphal procession down the Via Nationale from our hotel balcony. Police
inspected our rooms – but not our baggage, which was never
searched throughout our holiday – and told us to leave our
room door open. I took my camera on to the balcony and held
it so shakily that I nearly let the two dictators pass out of sight
before clicking the shutter. 'If only', I said to K, 'we had known
where to get a bomb.' It seems easy enough now to acquire
gelignite or at least petrol or nail bombs, but this was hardly
common knowledge in the 1930s. Whether I would have hurled
a bomb, whether I would have had the skill and courage to
throw it, whether I would have sacrificed K's life as well as
my own are absurdly academic questions – and yet intolerably
searching. If I had been able then to destroy Mussolini and
Hitler, would it have been *right*, given what I knew about the
evils of Fascism and Nazism then, which was plenty, let alone
what I knew later? I am pretty sure my courage would have
failed me, but I know now that if I had had the means and the

25

will I might have saved the lives of millions of Jews. Hitler, Himmler and Goering were so perverted and evil and had such monstrous power to pervert and corrupt masses of their fellow citizens that surely it would have been right to sacrifice one's conscience as well as one's life to extinguishing them? And yet, and yet . . . to admit the right of conscience to assassinate evil men is to leave too much to the judgement of the individual; to open the door to the assassins of John and Robert Kennedy, the assassins of many another head of state. Even Gandhi was assassinated. There are no valid answers to my questions, and in time of war the pacifist learns what a frail mentor conscience really is, for he compromises even by accepting food brought in by armed convoy.

Among our friends, when war broke out in 1939, two or three were conscientious objectors who accepted alternative forms of service and two or three accepted 'reservation' in their jobs even though they worked for newspapers which supported the war effort. Not one went to prison (conscientious objection was, of course, much more widely recognized as an honourable attitude than in World War I). K's position was that he could not justify conscientious objection but hoped by getting into the Navy to be more concerned in saving life than destroying it, and in fact served only on a destroyer on convoy in the Atlantic and on a mine-sweeping trawler corvette in the Mediterranean. I am thankful that he did not have to take on – or slough off – the burden of guilt for dropping bombs on civilian men, women or children, or hear the screams of any human being whom his action had maimed or killed. *Dulce et decorum est pro patria mori*. How have human beings been able to convince themselves, all these centuries, that that is what war is about? The ultimate sacrifice is not to die for some glorious abstract Cause, but to kill a child for it. Men, and women too, of the I.R.A. have the burden on their conscience of having been responsible for the death or maiming of children as well as inoffensive adults, by planting bombs in public places, justifying their actions by saying 'We are at war.' So have the members of many other fanatical nationalist groups. How can they fail to relate this justification of their small-scale bomb attacks to the justification that is always adduced for full-scale war – 'Civilian casualties are inevitable if we are to defeat the enemy'? Civilian casualties include *babies*. Is *any* cause, any threat to self-determination, worth that price? Since the invention of the atom bomb, at the touch of a switch hundreds of thousands of children, and their parents, could be obliterated. And for what? The idea that anything worth having could survive a global nuclear war is so obviously beyond credibility that it is a

26

wonder that heads of state do not sit down and look at themselves and ask, 'Are we all *mad*? How the nations of the world are to abstract themselves from the nuclear arms race is beyond my wits to see, but somehow I am able to believe that mankind's will to survive is stronger than his death wish.

I am not likely to live to see . . . but I remember . . . When, after Munich, the dreadful knowledge crept upon us that another world war was inevitable, what we were paralysingly afraid of was *gas*. We had been told over and over again that another war would not be like the last one – armies locked in mile upon mile of stinking trenches. J. B. S. Haldane and others had described vividly to us the horrors of mustard and other gases, and there were enough men still about whose health had been permanently wrecked by being gassed in the trenches. When the children were sent off to the country in September, 1939 to escape from what was thought to be inevitable, massed bombing, they carried pitiful little cardboard boxes containing gas masks round their necks. We all carried these totally inadequate snorkels around with us wherever we went, and I doubt whether they would have saved a single life; certainly they offered no protection against mustard gas burns. The gas threat never became an actuality. So when my young friends were frantic with worry for their children at the time of the threatened invasion of Cuba, I tried to calm them, especially my daughter. I had a sort of faith, and still have, that we shall draw back from the brink.

Perhaps if the Americans had suffered the hell of Dusseldorf or Coventry or the siege of Leningrad, they would not have been able to believe that their bombers could solve anything in Vietnam. Perhaps hope for the outlawing of war lies in the nations of Europe which have been devastated by it twice in my lifetime? Then why, I ask myself unhappily, did the Labour Party, which attracted me because I believed it to be the party of international brotherhood as well as of social justice, make so many difficulties about joining the European Community? Because, of course, it was envisaged as a trading community which would primarily benefit the international cartels and the big business interests, and because its advocacy had fallen into the hands of a Conservative prime minister. Naïve and sentimental my view of politics may be, but I think that if the Labour Party had been able to see this great imaginative leap forward into Europe predominantly as a long overdue reintegration of the culture we share with the French, the Germans, the Italians, an integration of *peoples* which might outlaw the possibility of another European holocaust, the British elector might have been coaxed along, rather than confirmed in the vice of chauvinism and encouraged to get neurotic about the price of butter and beef. But the Labour Party seems to have lost its concern about international brotherhood. It was a Labour government which refused to recognize as valid the British passports of the Kenya Asians, a shock to my political allegiance which has left me doubting whether I really belong anywhere in the political spectrum.

Yet every time a crisis has divided the nation I have had no doubt that I belonged with the Left, the underprivileged, rather than the Right, nor that one should, idealistically and optimistically, go on trying to make life easier, better, more enjoyable, safer, for more and more people. What dismays me about the times in which I write is that among the impatient and rebellious young, violence seems to have become respectable. It is safe to say that in my rebellious young days only committed Communists believed in the use of violence for political ends, and in this country they did not really practise it. Life was much beastlier for far more people in the twenties and thirties than for anyone today, and today's young rebels must not think there was no anger among us then. But not until Mosley's Fascists marched and held their Hitler-type rallies was there, in my recollection, anything much worse than verbal violence, rowdyism, persistent – though not organized – heckling. Mosley is an old man now, and they say old men forget. He seems to have convinced himself that he did not incite violence against hecklers or against the Jews, so I must record that after one of his rallies in the Free Trade Hall, Manchester, I heard as I was coming down the stairs one hefty Blackshirt call to another, 'Bump him. Bump him down the stairs.'

But never at any meeting I attended in those pre-war days did I hear the sort of barrage or stamping that makes it impossible for any speaker to carry on; I know there were scuffles between picketers and police during the miners' strike of 1926, but the sort of demonstration in which people, especially the young, eagerly engage now was not for us. There is, perhaps, a touch of absurdity in 'demo-itis' – when I took part, early in 1972, in a small picket of the *Punch* offices, protesting at the male exclusivity of the famous *Punch* lunch table, I was incredulous at the expenditure of public funds on a posse of police to control this group of thirty or forty self-conscious, placard-carrying women journalists. What did they think we were going to do? Tear the hair of our professional colleagues who saw fit to accept Mr Punch's invitation to an all-female lunch party? Most of us were giggling as we walked in file along the pavement escorted by those solemn bobbies, to the Fleet Street pub where we laid aside our little banners. It is, of course, partly because of the very real danger to the safety of masses of people processing through streets or gathering in public squares that Authority has accepted the equation 'demonstration equals violence', but the great Aldermaston marches proved that the will of the demonstrators to avoid violence is the greatest safety factor. But the police know, the mass media know, and demonstrators recognize, with some bitterness, that there is an *interest* in violent scuffles. It is the scuffles, the arrests, the baton charges that are photographed and written about, that make the only really effective propaganda for the Cause. It is frightening that to so many young people violent action seems not only acceptable but the only effective means of securing change. (Only, to keep a sense of proportion, let us never forget the Suffragettes. Out of a sense of rage and frustration very similar to that of the radical young today, they hurled bricks through plate-glass windows and set letter boxes and old buildings on fire.)

It is hard to bear the assumption of the radical young that they are the first generation to question the getting and spending values of society: to *care*. I think in a way we cared more bitterly and personally – because it was *our* friends and brothers and husbands and lovers who were subject to the humiliation of the means test and the dole, who really went short of food and clothes and medical care – than the young students maintained on fairly adequate grants at universities and colleges. But if the young ask us, as I think they are entitled to do, why we didn't unite in revolution against this cruel and unjust society, I think the answer is not only that most of us still believed that society could be changed from inside, but that we had far less confidence in ourselves. Whether or not young people today are braver, stronger and clearer-sighted than we were, they certainly start from a position of greater strength. I believe they have moved forward on our backs. It was out of our humiliation and deprivation that the Welfare State was born. It was World War II that moved the economy into a new cycle in which the 'crises' have been mini tremors compared with the financial earthquake which shook the western world in 1930, and earnings and social security benefits have been lifted to a level that truly justifies the term 'affluent society' compared with the days of the Slump. It is a matter of cold fact that society has changed and that the greatest change is in the lessening of fear. I was sitting with my parents-in-law listening to the radio, somewhere in the 1940s, when a large improvement in retirement pensions was announced. The relief on the face of my mother-in-law lives on in my mind. For the first time I realized that this proud, reserved, independent woman, who had three fine sons and a daughter, had been concealing a fear of dire poverty in old age, of total dependence on her children, which was none the less real because it was quite unjustified.

We who were young, rebellious and idealistic in the thirties had far too simplistic a view of society and of human nature. Most of us accepted the Fabian doctrine of the inevitability of gradualness. And we accepted also the view of the Webbs, of Shaw and Wells that if only men would use their native wits to organize society on a rational basis and remove the profit motive, human beings would cease to exploit each other, would work for the common good and cease to be beastly to one another. We thought – oh yes we did – that by nationalizing the essential industries we should give the workers in them the dignity and security of being partners in a great communal enterprise. We tended to believe in the perfectibility of man. What we didn't know about was the infinite corruptibility of man – that horrifying knowledge came at the time of Auschwitz, when apparently normally affectionate and decent husbands and fathers were found in ample numbers to herd millions of Jews in cattle trucks across Europe and to force them, men, women and children, into gas chambers.

It is not surprising that the Fabians, so confident of the force of reason, were blinded to the force of unreason, the power of the demagogue to play on fear and suspicion, to make the darkest strands in human nature, hatred and violence, respectable. What is surprising is that they closed their eyes to the maxim, 'Much wants more', for they very well understood that the really poor are inert, flaccid, apathetic and only when they are lifted out of absolute poverty will men have the will to fight. To abolish poverty was the most laudable of aims – but at what point are human beings able to say, 'Hold, enough'? We *have* abolished absolute poverty in the United Kingdom in the 1970s – even by the standards of the 1930s, let alone by the standard of starvation-level poverty endured around half the world. But we can see now that relative poverty stings much worse. Where does rebellion at our lot cease to be laudable and become selfish and greedy? In our times it is seldom intolerable hardship that causes strikes and the threat of strikes . . . it is bitterness at being undervalued in money terms compared with some other section of workers. Teachers, machine minders, surgeons, dockers, air-line pilots, dustmen, miners, car assembly workers, postmen, journalists, train drivers, all regard themselves as 'special cases' – because they have special skills, special responsibility, have specially intolerable conditions of work, are specially important to the economy; because they deserve more, *vis-à-vis* someone who works less hard, has less skill, less importance. There is no union leader, no representative of a professional body who would dare to stand up in front of his members and say, 'Wait a minute – we don't do so badly compared with . . . ' There is no organized body of workers who would be prepared to hold back a wage claim because some other workers deserve first place in the queue. Much wants more. We live in a very greedy society.

Yet I see a flicker of hope that we begin to understand. Despite the inconvenience, ordinary people were on the side of the striking postmen in 1971; by and large, despite great discomfort and even misery, ordinary people were on the side of the striking and picketing miners in 1972. That didn't mean that most of us were prepared to accept higher postal charges or a higher price for coal and electricity, or would not grumble furiously. It did mean a recognition that postmen and miners *deserved* more; that the value of their labour to the whole community was appreciated. I doubt if the miners could have won their claim if during those candlelit days the mood of the ordinary people had changed to anger. Only a tiny flicker of hope of a willingness to make sacrifices for other people's good – but there are other indications of change, especially among the young. No one who talks to students can be unaware of a mood quite different from the angry battling for 'rights' and 'power' which is what we chiefly read about. I had an example of this new mood when taking part in the B.B.C. radio programme 'Question of Belief' at Manchester University Institute of Science and Technology. We members of the platform panel asked the students – the management men, technicians and scientists of the future – whether they saw their careers mainly in terms of their own advancement or in terms of service to the community. All the students who came to the microphone said 'service to the community' and we were left in no doubt that the anger these young people felt was not against being bossed around by faceless Authority so much as being caught up into a remorseless 'rat race'.

We who are old know that youthful idealism cools . . . but if only a few of today's crop of students go out into the world to do battle against the rat race – the getting and spending values of our society, produce more, consume more, grab more for yourself – their alternative values will work as a yeast. And in fact I believe this yeast is already working and that more and more people are being forced to ask themselves whether it makes sense to clutter up the earth with more and more goods, to denude its natural resources, pollute its atmosphere and threaten the survival of our children. Within the last two or three years we have begun to see even the motor car as a symbol not of twentieth-century success but of twentieth-century failure. Fewer people now preach the gospel of 'the more cars the better' for the satisfaction of the individual and the prosperity of the nation; more preach the gospel that the car is the enemy of the quality of life in an overpopulated island. It is polluting the atmosphere, choking up the cities, causing death and injury, eating up what remains of our beautiful countryside – and above all it is the symbol of a greedy society's unwillingness to accept limitations on individual freedom for the common good. The car lobby is powerful, the Concorde lobby is powerful, the Third Airport lobby and the North Sea Oil lobby, but even since I began to write this book concern for the quality of life has strengthened and spread. I have some hope that we are feeling our way to a brave new world in which our children may hope to live more peacefully and rewardingly.

So towards the end of my long journey I am not drowned in gloom. I see all about me evidences that there is a will to survive; a will to opt in to a new kind of society as much as a will to opt out of the old; a willingness to participate in 'do-it-yourself' activities from communes and underground newspapers to Citizen's Advice Bureaux and Pre-School Playgroups, Claimants' Unions, women's houses for battered wives, to offset against the disenchantment with hidebound parliamentary procedures; a much wider acceptance of the need for social justice, to offset against the increase in violent agitation. Of all the changes I have seen the one which gives me most comfort and hope is the very real progress towards an egalitarian society. Of course it is still better to be born into an upper-class family whose children automatically go to public schools than into the family of a dustman whose children attend crummy, overcrowded, understaffed primary and secondary schools. But only a diminishing minority of our fellow-citizens now thinks that this is *right*, or even, for all time, inevitable, much less divinely ordained; only a diminishing handful now sneers at a 'working-class accent' or accepts intellectually that it is the mark of an inferior person, though it may indeed still be a handicap in dealing with people invested with a little authority. Read Trollope, if you doubt whether we have come far in the last century along the road to an integrated society. With all its gaps and flaws and failures, the Welfare State is based on the assumption that every member of the community has the basic right not only to care and maintenance in need, but to the opportunity to fulfill his potential. Trollope, though a generous, liberal, tolerant sort of man was incapable of imagining that the son of a docker might be of intrinsically greater worth and of more value to society than the son of a duke. Isn't it some gain that that now seems a self-evident truth? And that no child is expected to sing, as I was, that shocking verse from the jolly hymn 'All Things Bright and Beautiful'?:

> *The rich man in his castle*
> *The poor man at his gate*
> *God made them high or lowly*
> *And ordered their estate.*

3. NEWSPRINT IN THE NOSTRILS

In April, 1925, aged nearly eighteen, I presented myself in the readers' room of the old *Leicester Mail*. It was the size of a boxroom and it smelled of stale food, because the chief reader, Fatty Prest, kept sandwiches too long in his desk drawer. He was flabby-fat and sallow, with a drooping black moustache, and he had a fine pompous way of reading copy, articulating every syllable and every punctuation mark. Exclamation marks were strike-'em-stiffs. I have been told that other readers call them dogs' piddlers and even coarser terms.

As, being female, I could not belong to the Typographical Association or the Association of Correctors of the Press, I should not really have been in the readers' room at all, but I was tolerated as a strictly temporary copyholder. This meant that Clarence, a neat, dark, adenoidal youth, read aloud from the galley proof and I had to follow the original, often abominably handwritten copy, and speak up if the written and printed words did not tally. Even in those lax times there would have been trouble if I had actually marked the proofs, but Fatty Prest was a fatherly man, anxious to teach me what he could, and he let me take away proofs of non-urgent copy, like the stock prices and 'form of the horses' and correct them at home. I don't remember being bored by any of it, except the racing, and to help that along I used to make bets with myself. On Derby Day I placed a real bet. Being earnest and priggish I was quite ashamed of my win and never placed a bet again. That fusty little readers' box was a good place to get the feel of how newspapers are put together.

My very first night on the *Mail* I had a job, Miss Constance

33

Hardcastle's pupils' concert. Naturally my mother went too, but she left me alone to write. Picturing my metaphorical wet cloth round my brow, I was prepared to sit up all night to compose my masterpiece, and I was faintly disappointed that I had completed it in an hour or so. It went into the paper word for word as I had written it. You could say that Uncle Harry, my sponsor, who was chief sub-editor of the *Leicester Mail*, art critic, theatre critic, music critic, sole leader writer, was kindly disposed to his sister's child, but he was an unsentimental man. In *Leicester Mail* terms, in 1925, the notice was passable. As my daughter's notice of the Rome fashion collections written unaided for the *Guardian* when she was only sixteen was more than passable. The basic knack is there and how it started seems to me an awe-inspiring mystery. That doctors marry doctors and breed doctors, journalists marry journalists and breed journalists, is not surprising, for the environmental factor is potent. But somewhere back in the genetic chain there was a sport, there was a founding father, or mother.

In our case it was William Taylor Bates, my mother's father. We were told as children that William Bates came of Essex fisherfolk so poor that he was scaring birds for a few pence a week when he was a boy; that he carried ashore his future bride, Charlotte Jonsen, when she came across the North Sea from Denmark. (She was born a Dane and, after the conquest of Schleswig Holstein, reared a German.) Vater Bates (we, as well as their seven children, called our grandparents Vater and Mutter) became, goodness knows how, a miller, and when I first remember him was managing a flour mill in Nuneaton, Warwickshire. He was Viking-tall, blond-bearded, fiercely radical, terrifying to children ('Get out of my light, boy'; 'Sit up, girl, look at your mother') and contumacious (I came into our sitting-room once to hear him bawling 'Claptrap' to the radio). He was always writing Letters to the Editor, especially to Henry Labouchere's *Truth*, and articles for the trade press. When he retired from the mill he became editor of *The Miller*. My other grandfather, Thomas Peirce Waddington, was a printer, and used to write the occasional concert notice.

Two of the Bates children became journalists, the oldest, my mother, Amalie Maria Christina Bates and the second son, Henry Edward. Malie married, so to speak, into the business, for though she and my father, Robert Guy Waddington, had started life as elementary school teachers, when they met my father was running in his spare time a weekly newspaper in Leicester, *The Wyvern*, which his father printed. He persuaded my mother to write a women's column for it, as 'Priscilla'.

Perhaps that was what set the younger brother off, but all those talented Bates brothers and sisters had the knack of words. Bob became a full-time journalist with the *Leicester Morning Post* and *Leicester Mercury* in World War I, and Malie wrote her women's columns for them. Uncle Harry went off to the *Bombay Times* but had returned to be a Pooh-Bah at the *Leicester Mail* when I came into the story.

Sub-editing staffs were very small in those far-off days, and most of Uncle Harry's fell ill at the same time. He contacted my mother, then irritably 'resting'. 'You'll have to come and help me.' 'What, me? I don't know anything about subbing.' 'You can learn.' And of course she did . . . possibly the first woman news sub in the country. At this time a very odd thing happened to me. In the sixth form at the Wyggeston Grammar School for Girls I was all set to take a high-powered secretarial course which I hoped would get me to Geneva to work for the League of Nations. Up to that point I had never considered journalism as a career. But we were set to write an essay on newspapers, and writing it I had a Call, as real and urgent as a nurse's, even a nun's. There is no explaining why it hadn't happened before, or why it happened then. Just a fermenting of the yeast in my system, you might say. And because of the unlikely chance that the editor of the *Leicester Mail* owed my mother a favour, I was taken on as a copyholder for three months at ten shillings a week and then moved down to the reporters' room.

It seems to me now that I never really learned to be a reporter. My memories are more of washing up the chief reporter's teacup, writing copy at the reporters' dictation and being teased by them with horrific stories of the body in Braunstone Wood, than of producing news stories. The chief reporter suffered grievously from arthritis and his hands were so bent that often he could scarcely hold a pen. So on Tuesday mornings he would call me to his room, hand me the programme of the local variety theatre, indicate what the various turns were about, and turn over the writing of the notice to me. I had often also done three cinemas, two on my own account, and one extra if any of the men wanted to sit through a whole programme with his girl friend. But I did at the age of about eighteen write a notice of Pavlova dancing in the De Montfort Hall without having the slightest notion that I might have been a bit young for the job. 'Her dancing is like blown thistledown or a fallen leaf caught in the wind.' 'No one can witness her greatest triumph, "The Swan" without a sensation of almost eerie sadness!' But what I really liked was to make 'the calls', a tour of police stations and fire stations; going to inquests and the police court, accompanied at first and then on my own, and later, being one of the team reporting the city council meetings. Weddings I always loathed, even riding to them on the back of a photographer's motor bicycle. Once, writing up a wedding from the hand-out sheet we sent to brides, I got it into the paper a day too soon. I suppose it still happens.

Perhaps I might have made a good hard news reporter if I had been given time, but I wasn't. I was only nineteen when a new editor called me to his room and broke my heart by telling me I was to take over the women's page. I scarcely exaggerate. It *was* a heartbreak, for I thought my chance of becoming a 'real journalist' was finished. I have often wondered why it happened. To save money? There was no union salary scale for the under-twenties then and my starting salary was twenty-five shillings a week. Was it because my predecessor, fired to make room for me, was a bit of a bore? She may have been, but though I might perhaps have been regarded as a bright lass, I was hardly, at that age, equipped to inform and entertain the matrons of Leicester. Perhaps the idea was that for twenty-five bob a week the paper would get the services of mother as well as daughter, and indeed, mother did supply me with recipes, after my carelessly copying out someone else's recipe in which I had specified two *tablespoonfuls* of ginger for a cake. I raged over being expected to have a knowledge of the domestic arts and fashion, in which I was not at all interested. Looking back I realize that what I actually did, writing nice little paragraphs about bazaars and women's institutes and meetings and personalities, suited me quite well. Knocking on doors and ferreting for information people didn't want to give would have scared me. And as a compensation for doing women's stuff, I was allowed to do theatre. 'Jacques', I called myself, and thought I was pretty good. Like almost every journalist you could name, my ambition then was to be a topline theatre critic.

When and how did I get it into my head that the sum of all ambition was to be a chief sub-editor? Perhaps it started with a love affair I had with type faces, which sprang from a sort of love affair with a brilliant typographer who came to us from the old *Sunday Worker*. He prodded me out of my bourgeois priggishness and my sentimental religiosity and he taught me how to *see* type. I started to devise my own lay-outs and go up into the composing room – 'on the stone' we call it – to see the page assembled. These were very happy hours. The comps teased me and taught me. If I was 'Miss Waddington' then the deft-fingered comp at the other side of the stone, cheerfully leading out half a column to make it fit, had to be 'Mr Smith'. We had great respect and affection for one another. After I had left the *Mail* my brother, who had followed me on to its staff, reported that when he had difficulty in making a page fit, a comp said to him, 'You should send for your sister.' No accolade has ever pleased me more. Forty years later when in my so-called 'retirement' I spent some months as caretaker-editor of the *Observer* women's pages, I found that nothing I had learned about type and make-up had been forgotten. I could stand at the stone as confident of knowing how to make every-thing fit as if I had been handling type all my working life. In the *Observer* composing room I was 'Mary' to everyone, and the men on the other side of the stone who teased and joked with me were George, Dick, Alan, Charlie, and so on, to me. I found the freshly-inked silvery type as beautiful as in my apprentice years. I was very happy – at least as happy, strange as it may seem, as in having completed a well-turned article or organizing a well-balanced flow of copy for the pages. I never subbed a line of anyone else's copy in Leicester, and yet this conviction was growing in me that the subs room was where I belonged. I can only think that seeing the pages assembled I felt that this was where the power lay, the power to select and cut and amalgamate all the threads of the paper into one viable whole. It was the *newspaper* I loved, not just my bit of it or anyone else's bit. I saw the chief sub-editor as the spider in the web, the wizard with the wand, the Grand Vizier. It was a daft ambition for a girl in those days. Some people still think it daft.

What I feel now about those six years on the *Leicester Mail* was that a lot of my time was frittered. I wish I had been through a harder, more disciplined school. In those days it was a harum scarum kind of place, sloppily run. Drunks and lay-abouts were tolerated. There were late-night parties when we were supposed to be writing our overnight copy, to which one of us brought his dim boy friends, and another, an Irish drunk, brought a gramophone he had got on tick, and to which we danced around the reporters' room. We were almost all very young and very Left. Our harassed editor had to try to call us to order during the General Election of 1929. We were, after all, owned by the local Conservative and Unionist Association.

It all sounds great fun, the sort of gay amateurism with which *Private Eye*, *Time Out*, *Oz* started – cocking a snook at our Tory masters, the enthusiasm for writing, the light-hearted irrespon-sibility to news. Henri Rosen used to invent 'news' and would sometimes get an invented running story into the paper day after day. I think it was only fun in parts, because the framework was not firm enough even to rebel against with conviction; cer-tainly not firm enough to force me into professional, emotional or political maturity. And of course, we were skittering about

37

on the surface of an economic quagmire, whose depth and extent it was hard to realize in Leicester, which never suffered mass unemployment. The poor old *Leicester Mail* was, in 1931, sliding into bankruptcy, and no one knew, from week to week, who would be fired. In February my mother died and this must have given the harassed editor an excuse to get rid of me – I could be usefully employed staying at home and looking after my father and unmarried brother. I was probably too numb from shock to take in how perilous my future was. It was my brave, good father who, at the time of the 1931 census, insisted that I should be described as 'journalist, unemployed', not 'housewife'. It was he who scoured the papers for job advertisements and found the one that took me, only a few weeks later, to the *Bolton Evening News.*

There couldn't have been two more different newspaper atmospheres than the *Leicester Mail* and the *Bolton Evening News.* In Bolton the offices were positively stately. The reporters were all worthy citizens who went home for a one and a half hour lunchbreak, leaving the office practically deserted. No drunks, no Commies, no eccentrics. The test of a good reporter, it seemed to me, was to be able to turn in a good column report of a meeting, and this happily, despite rather shaky shorthand, I was able to do, winning much approval for reporting meetings as well as writing personal paragraphs about them for my weekly 'women's diary'.

Not only the office, but the whole town, then in the depths of the Slump, seemed to me deathly quiet. It was hard to find enough going on to fill even a weekly 'diary', whereas in Leicester I had easily found enough to fill a daily column. In newspaper terms I was marking time, but the orderly atmosphere was a blessing at a time when my personal life was extremely unhappy – I was burdened with a relationship which drained me financially as well as in every other way, and after a year my father also died. It was a pretty grim time, but I made lifelong friends in Bolton and I learned a lot about what local newspapers mean to the democratic process, from the editor, Isaac Edwards, who was one of the most able, vigorous and effective journalists I have ever known, though he never moved out of his home town.

Ike's abrupt, sardonic manner, his fierce eyebrows, his bellow, were terrifying at first. He said that shouting had become a habit because deafness seemed to be hereditary among the Tillotsons who owned the paper. He would burst into my room and fire questions at me – but once I had learned to answer back smartly, even pertly, we got on to very good terms and my affection for him came to match my admiration. His good mind could certainly have taken him to Fleet Street, but he chose to stay in Bolton because he cared about it, belonged to it, wanted to serve it. Men like Ike keep alive a sense of involvement in local government. His successor, Frank Singleton, a bright young reporter in my time in Bolton, understood this very well. He went up to Cambridge late, became President of the Union, moved to London and earned the friendship of some of the best-known authors of our day. But when, after Ike's death, the editorship of the *Bolton Evening News* was offered to him, I think he was proud to accept it. Lancashire men still tend to be more conscious of their roots than most of us. K, also born in Bolton, was of the same kind.

But for me, two years in Bolton were enough. I applied for the job of editing the women's and children's publications of the Co-operative Press in Manchester. To my alarm, after an initial interview, the directors sent a deputation to check my credentials and suitability with my editor. When they left, Ike came into my room beaming. 'I told them 101 per cent,' he said. So I was interviewed again, by the full board – I think there were at least ten of them – and I think what probably clinched my getting the job was my saying, 'I've always wanted to work for a cause as well as a paper.' And work for a cause I did, sincerely and devotedly, for twelve good years. The co-operative principle seemed then, still seems to me, basic to civilization, so the propaganda element in our work was a welcome opportunity, not a burden. What I was responsible for was the two pages of the weekly *Co-operative News* devoted mainly to reports of the activities of the Women's Co-operative Guild, the fortnightly (later weekly) *Women's Outlook*, a little magazine in the small-page old *Home Chat* format, the monthly children's magazine *Our Circle*, the monthly *Co-operative Youth*, organ of the co-operative movement's youth movement, and the monthly *Sunshine Stories* for the tinies.

There was a staff of two women journalists and a secretary. I was twenty-six, Nora Crossley two years older, Rose Simpson ten years older and the secretary, Margaret Foster, about the same age as I. There were hints at my interview with the board of directors, when I was sounded as to whether I was an 'amiable' sort of character, that I was walking into a 'situation' but I was not, of course, told that both Nora and Rose were contenders for the job, Nora very rightly and naturally, since she had been assistant to my predecessor, Mrs Annie Bamford Tomlinson, and Rose out of a sense of Socialist mission and also raging personal ambition. All three of them disliked one another heartily and I had been brought in as a solvent. Nora and I respected one another and became lasting friends. I tried pathetically hard to make a friend also of Rose Simpson, but her envy and sense of frustration had become pathological. The effect of somewhat lessening her overt hostility to me was to intensify her hostility to the secretary. There was a day when Rose and I sat in the room of the editor, James Flanagan, and she said in the voice of a Sarah Bernhardt, 'To think that I have looked at these hands and thought they might do murder.' There was another when Rose said, 'If I had been willing to be the editor's mistress I would have had your job.' (She was large and imposing and he small and dapper.) My knees gave and I flopped into a chair on the verge of hysteria. Another day she swept out of the office announcing her intention to commit suicide. No one else took her seriously, but I went through some very bad hours until I could establish that she was safely at home.

Poor Rose. She became, not without assistance, I am ashamed to say, from Nora Crossley and me, general secretary of the Women's Co-operative Guild, in succession to Eleanor Barton, and her megalomania grew to the point where the central committee, very bravely, decided to fire her. It was a tragic case of a not very good brain housed in a very powerful personality. It was not a very easy situation for a young woman still in her twenties to cope with.

But the job itself was all right. There was no money to spend on the publication so we did everything. The *Co-operative News* and all the magazines were sold only through the co-operative movement, the retail societies and the ancillary organizations, almost always at a small loss. So we wrote almost every word ourselves, apart from the fiction for *Woman's Outlook* which we bought in the cheapest syndicated market. In fact Nora Crossley and I wrote several serial stories ourselves. She also kept up a marvellous flow of 'Tales from the Opera' and such for *Our Circle*. I wrote the lives of pioneer feminists for *Woman's Outlook*. Rose did some good work in the trade union field. We wrote our cookery from other people's recipes, and pinched our illustrations from other magazines, painting out the bits that didn't fit our purpose. We all did our own make-up, of course, and went in for some stunning fancy work on *Woman's Outlook* in the way of cut-out pictures and indented type. This meant that we had to measure both words and pictures very accurately for our small page size, and I still find it difficult to be patient with people who when asked, 'How much have you written?' say, 'Oh about eight paras' or 'About two and a half pages' – about as helpful as saying, 'Oh about as long as a piece of string.'

We also reported a great many conferences for the *Co-*

operative News which improved my shorthand wonderfully and brought me into close personal touch with the splendid women of the co-operative movement from whom I learned so much. Within two or three weeks of joining the Co-operative Press I had to cover, with Nora Crossley and Tom Mercer of our London staff, the jubilee conference of the Women's Co-operative Guild, which meant wiring off thousands of words for the *Co-operative News*. It was a scaring, but exhilarating start. I never ceased to find this annual congress moving, and reporters from the Press Association and local papers who came to scoff often stayed to marvel.

So I learned a great deal at the Co-operative Press – about working-class attitudes and achievements; about the technique of producing newspapers and magazines; about writing simply and unpedantically; about the initiation of and receptivity to ideas which is the key to editing. The one drawback was that journalistically the Co-operative Press was cut off from the mainstream. I often wondered restlessly how I would measure up against 'real' journalists. Our main contact with 'The Street of Adventure' was *Reynolds News,* later the *Sunday Citizen*, and its remarkable first editor, Sydney Elliott. *Reynolds News*, unlike the *Guardian* which also moved into Gray's Inn Road, was never more than on the fringe of Fleet Street, and unlike the *News Chronicle*, whose death is still mourned, it sank almost without trace. I never hear it mentioned even by the distinguished journalists whom it cradled. But there was a time when that energetic, inventive, driving man Alfred Barnes, chairman of the Co-operative Press board and of the Co-operative Party, and that brilliant political writer and speaker, Sydney Elliott, very nearly brought it to success. In this time Alfred Barnes's conference of editors, held in the House of Commons, considerably enhanced my sense of status and involvement, and Sydney, dear romantic Sydney whose tall stories I swallowed almost whole, was like a kingfisher in a world of colourless sparrows. Beaverbrook enticed him away to edit the *Evening Standard* in 1942. Later he edited the *Daily Herald*, and as political adviser to the *Daily Mirror* claimed to have invented the election-winning slogan 'Vote for Him' at the end of the war. Alfred Barnes slipped into retirement and so did Sydney. I wish I knew why.

Actually the Co-operative Press felt much less like a backwater when James Flanagan, the editor when I was appointed, retired and Bill Richardson 'our man in Newcastle' took charge of the Manchester publications. Jimmy was a real journalist and a delightful man – his pseudonym, 'Myles Long', indicates his sense of fun. I believe it was he who inspired the Co-operative

41

Press's purchase of the decrepit *Reynolds News*. But by the time I arrived he had come to prefer lunchtime conviviality to hard work. Bill, a shrewd, energetic, slightly rakish Geordie, got us all organized. I like organization men. I like being an organization woman. We got on fine. When the war broke out and the staff was depleted, I became more and more involved with the *Co-operative News* and was able to leave the women's side almost entirely to my faithful colleague and friend Nora Crossley. I made up news pages and wrote leaders as well as leader page articles and after a while began to preside at the weekly editorial conference when Bill was away. K was called up into the Navy, bombs fell on Manchester, the windows of the grim old Co-operative Press office in Long Millgate were blown out and fires raged all around on the nights of the twenty-second and twenty-third of December, 1941; but professionally I was having a splendid time. After K went off for his Navy training, Bill would say to me, 'You've no home to go to. Let's stay on and finish this job' – and then he would take me on a small pub crawl. K was glad for me. Unlike many men, he did not want his wife to be a 'camp follower'. All the years he was in the Navy he clung to the knowledge that I was there, in our home, carrying on the sort of life we had always lived together, remaining the same kind of person; that his home, and his wife, would be there when, by the grace of God, he came back.

But when Bill – how hard it is to think of him now as Sir William Richardson – succeeded Sydney Elliott as editor of *Reynolds News* in 1942, the only obvious candidate who was available was me – and I was female. Bill told me afterwards, 'There's no doubt you would have got it if you had worn trousers.' What actually happened was that one of the directors whom I counted as a friend and was particularly 'pro women' happened to meet the then general secretary of the Co-operative Union, Robert Palmer (Lord Rusholme), on the morning of the decisive board meeting. 'It would be a bit awkward for Mary, wouldn't it', said Bob, 'dealing with the men from the C.W.S. and Co-op Union?' So one vote I had counted on as certain was switched and cost me the job.

Actually, it was a good thing. Unknown to anyone except K and my close family I was pregnant, after five years of longing for a child. It was my not being assessed on my merits as a journalist that wounded me and the scar took quite a long while to heal. It is forgotten and forgiven now, for thirty years after my rejection a more enlightened Co-operative Press board did appoint a woman, Mrs Lily Howe, to edit the *Co-operative News* – an excellent choice. And actually, in 1943 it was the greatest good luck to be able to take time off to have the baby and return to a quiet office where I knew the ropes, could get home for lunch and to breast-feed the child, and earn enough money to maintain the family while K was on an able seaman's pay. During the two very bloody years he was in the Mediterranean it was the Co-operative Press – and, of course, my joy in the child – that just about made life bearable. More women now than then will understand what I mean. I had already been a journalist for eighteen years. My work was as much me as being a mother. Being a mother was as much me as being a journalist. I could not have split myself in half. When Tom Henry, editor of the *Manchester Evening News*, said to me, 'Of course, you are a career woman, Mary,' I was outraged. No, never a career woman in the sense of forging ahead regardless of what my husband and daughter needed of me, or I needed of them. But K Stott's devoted wife, Catherine Stott's devoted mother, was also Mary Waddington, journalist.

For two years I worked on reasonably contented at the Co-operative Press, and produced a best-selling pamphlet, 'The People in Business', setting out the philosophy and purpose of the co-operative movement as I saw it, but by the time the war came to an end I was chafing at the bit. I had learned so much about getting out newspapers that the thought of going back to 'women's work' was intolerable. K was invalided home from the Mediterranean, with thyro-toxicosis, in May 1945, and with his encouragement I applied for a job as a news sub-editor on the *Manchester Evening News*. And got it. It was an astonishing appointment. It could scarcely have happened except at the tail end of the war when so many good men were still in the Forces and almost anyone experienced in handling copy was a rare asset, but the real luck was that the then editor of the *Evening News*, John Beavan (Lord Ardwick), was one of the few journalists at that time who was totally devoid of sex prejudice. He knew something about my experience with the co-operative movement, too, for his mother, Mrs Emily Beavan, was the president of the Women's Co-operative Guild jubilee congress at which I had made my *Co-operative News* debut. He appointed me specifically to handle home politics, including Parliament, and so began five of the most exhilarating years of my professional life. The dream had not been a delusion.

It is difficult to explain to 'writing' journalists, let alone to a non-newspaper person, the excitement I found working in the sub-editors' room. Perhaps a woman engineer working on the site may understand it better, for one element was undoubtedly being able to do a job that men had always assumed women couldn't do. Women engineers could understand, too, the satisfaction of mastering a fairly complicated technique. What do sub-editors do, for heaven's sake, except cut bits out and write headlines? Basically, they get the news into the paper, edition by edition, and make it fit. They battle for seven or eight hours a day, or night, with the two implacable enemies, time and space. The crucial thing about putting newspapers together is, as a head printer used to say to me, that type is not made of indiarubber. There are so many inches to a column length and so many ems to a column width and the page cannot be locked up and wheeled away for the matrix and stereo plates to be made until it precisely fits. So the wittiest headline in the world is useless if it is one letter, or even half a letter, too wide when it is set in type. The most vivid and perceptive piece of reporting must be trimmed, carefully and intelligently one hopes, so as not to run off the bottom of the page. That brilliant exclusive news story may be arriving, folio by folio, minutes before the edition time. It *must* be carefully read, for even the most distinguished reporter can make slips – or, more likely, can be misheard by the telephone copytaker – and it must have a heading that will not 'bounce', or the page will be delayed while it comes back from the composing room to be altered.

All newspapers have headline codes which are not only an indication to the sub-editor handling them as to how many letters he can get into his headline, but a fairly rigid guide as to the length he can let the story run – from twenty-five words to a column or more. How else could a page plan be made to fit? There must be a 'splash', or page lead, so many 'tops', so many 'down-page doubles', and a good supply of short stories which are expendable. Writing headings to fit and cutting stories to length becomes fairly easy with practice. As a crossword puzzle addict can usually solve an anagram at a glance, so can the experienced sub-editor usually produce quickly a combination of words that will add up to sixteen, twenty, or whatever, letters and spaces. (Not quite so easy as it sounds, however, if you remember that some large-type single column headings will take a maximum of seven letters to a line.) The real battle, though, is with what we call a 'running story' – a major news event where the situation is changing all day, or all night, long. There will be an endless flow of 'snaps', 'flashes' and full stories, from the Press Association, Reuters and the other news agencies, stories from staff reporters and correspondents, fluttering on to the sub's desk. He must instantly decide what is new and significant, yell for a messenger to get it to the composing room to be set for the Stop Press or inserted into the story, and discard the rest. Always with an eye on the clock, and always 're-jigging' the story in time for the next edition so that it reads smoothly; containing both the latest news and the earlier news which is stale to him but still new to the reader who buys the paper on the way home from work or reads it over the breakfast table. 'On Time Means On Sale' and 'Trains Won't Wait', the *Manchester Evening News* daily edition-time sheets used to exhort us.

I got to be rather good at this swift cutting and piecing, this remorseless battle with the clock – partly because I continued to handle Parliament, which meant a breathless rush to get Question Time into our Last Extra edition and the start of a big debate into the Final. I handled every kind of story except, thankfully, the most gruesome murders; I even got to be quite useful on Saturday afternoons subbing Cheshire League matches, once I had got into my head the Rugby League scoring system and could check the total of points. I subbed happily stories about multiple births and willingly took the fashion stories off the backs of the men. I acquired the confidence to shuffle out of sight what I called 'the dirty Rs' – small, unimportant, sordid sex cases – until I could safely spike them with the discarded copy at the end of the day. But the really good days were when the flow of copy was a deluge. On such a day a colleague, Len Harton, subbing a dock strike, got up to leave the room. The chief sub called out to him, 'The Lords have ended the Emergency.' 'Not mine, they haven't,' said Harton and sat down again.

When I was young, men including my brother John used to say to me of my ambition to be a sub-editor, 'You couldn't stand the pace; you couldn't stand the language.' Johnny would be surprised to know what language I can stand now, but I can vow, hand on heart, that in my five years at the *Manchester Evening News* I never heard a word to make me blush. Perhaps the men were gallantly holding themselves back, but I doubt it, and if they were, it didn't do them any harm and they didn't resent it. More than twenty years later a newspaper editor answering a questionnaire about women's employment sent out by the Women in Media group commented, 'Subbing is not suitable for women. The pace is too hectic.' But my *Manchester Evening News* colleagues knew I could stand the pace as well as they could; they knew because so many of the really sticky, taxing stories came my way. I have never liked attributing virtues and vices to one sex or the other, and yet I feel that, whether by nature or nurture, some women are particularly fitted for subbing. We tend to be patient and meticulous, and an essential, absolutely vital, part of subbing is checking. A sub who doesn't immediately reach for a reference book or call for cuttings when he is not quite sure of the spelling of a name, the meaning of a word, the accuracy of a title, isn't worth his

45

money and may be a liability. Women tend to have a feeling for pattern and so enjoy and are often very good at page lay-out. (I doubt if it is just by chance that there have been so many outstanding women crystallographers, a science which, if I understand it correctly, depends on the analysis of shapes and patterns.) And keeping one's cool when the heavens open and copy rains down from every quarter isn't unlike the ability a woman at home develops in keeping a grip when the door bell rings as the milk boils over, the toddler demands the pot and the awful thought strikes her that her husband asked her to phone the garage urgently. I am pretty certain that it was being able to keep my head, see the wood for the trees and grasp essentials quickly that made me a rather better than averagely good sub-editor. I have only written a handful of witty head-lines in my life and envy this delicious skill, but give me a wodge of flatulent, over-written, sloppily-thought-out copy and despite groans and curses I will patiently prune it to length and knock it into shape. If every journalist had spent a year or two in the subs room of an evening newspaper he would evaluate the worth of his stories a great deal more accurately – and modestly. He might also, like me, think that 1,000 words is as much as you can expect anyone to read over breakfast or tea on any subject unless it is of compelling interest.

It was a marvellous five years I spent in the subs room at the *Manchester Evening News*, despite the noise – telephones ring-ing, subs shouting 'BOY', harassed copytakers over the other side of the floor getting shriller and shriller as they tried to cope with bad telephone lines – despite the fatigue and the being stuck in one chair, at one desk, with only a very brief lunch break in the canteen, for eight hours a day. It got better and better when the men came home from the war, for most of them were first-class technicians and first-class human beings. It is absolutely wrong to think of 'the man with the blue pencil' (whoever used a blue pencil on a newspaper?) as a cold-blooded, dried-up philistine. Some sub-editors, like K, never write a line, but to think of them as uncreative is ludicrous. They are an essential factor in *creating the paper*. I know a sub who calls all copy 'stuff'. But he knows good 'stuff' from bad 'stuff'; he knows what people want to read, he has an uncanny sense of smell for what is phoney, doubtful or libellous. I found K's nose for libel aston-ishing. It seemed almost like a sixth sense. The chief sub-editor or night editor is to a newspaper what a director is to a film. I would rather have had that job than have written ten best sellers.

It will be a long time before that job comes a woman's way. At the *Manchester Evening News* all the new recruits were

46

seated by me. 'Miss Waddington's Guide to Sub-editors', scribbled on copy paper, was passed around until it almost fell apart. After a while, through seniority, I took my turn on Saturdays as 'copy-taster', whose function is to sift the incoming copy, handing out the lesser items, marked with headline styles, to the subs around the table, and passing on the major items to the chief sub-editor. After a few weeks my name was dropped from the duty rota. 'Why?' I asked the chief sub. 'Don't I measure up?' 'It was the editor's decision,' he said. So, with his approval, I went to the editor, Tom Henry. Tom was honest and explicit. 'We have to safeguard the succession, Mary, and the successor has to be a man.' So I had to go. To help to teach boys their job and have them jumped over you to a position where they have to give you instructions is not tolerable. The absurd thing is that Tom thinks I am a very good journalist. The nice thing is that we retain a considerable affection for one another, based on mutual respect. He was a masterly organizer – his instructions to the troops on Budget Day or at a General Election were superb – and his sense of what the man in the pub wants to read was faultless. Tom's *Evening News* had no intellectual pretensions. It was run on a shoestring and the quality of its feature articles was often painfully low. But it had a vulgar vitality and it sold well. It made quite a lot of money to help prop up the *Guardian*. I often brag about having worked for it.

I made one more attempt to escape from women's journalism, by becoming Town Hall reporter for the old *Daily Dispatch* in Manchester, but it wasn't a success. I used to sit in the bleak Press Room in the Town Hall, miserably wondering how to fill in time, since my sources of information were limited to the official contacts with the council committees, and I had not acquired the know-how to dig up information for myself. I was rather glad to 'retire' for a while in the autumn of 1950. Our nanny-housekeeper decided without warning to retire to North Wales. We had had such a miserable time with unsatisfactory helpers before she came that I decided to try domesticity myself. Just to be on the safe side, I got myself a very tiny job at the Co-operative Press on two days a week, and in a year or two this grew into a substantial part-time job, for I was asked to take on the editorship of the *Woman's Outlook* again. And in January, 1957, I started, as it were, a new career as editor of the women's page of the *Guardian*. With a new name, too – no longer Mary Waddington, but Mary Stott.

4. THE GREAT
GUARDIAN

When I walked into Room 6 of the New Corridor of the *Manchester Guardian* in Cross Street on a January morning in 1957, to start work as virtual, though not titular women's page editor, it was as quiet as a chapel on a weekday; not a soul within shouting distance. There was, typically, no one to welcome me, yet, also typically, a silent welcome had been organized. On my desk there was a new blotting pad, a portable typewriter, a paste pot and a beautiful pair of long scissors. When in March, 1969, I took my place on the *Guardian* floor of Thomson House, Gray's Inn Road, London, I squeezed into a small desk interlocking with a dozen or so others, with hardly two feet of space between each. Typewriters clacked fore and aft, telephones were seldom silent, everyone became involved in every one else's conversations. The noise, the lack of space, natural light and air, and above all, of privacy, appalled me. Yet after a year I knew I had no wish to go back to my splendid isolation. I, like the *Guardian*, had been dragged protesting into a new era. So perhaps from my limited viewpoint as women's page editor I can help to chart the transition from the great *Manchester Guardian* to the great national *Guardian* and indicate how it was born, survived its birth pangs and transformed itself.

A. P. Wadsworth, fourth editor of the *Manchester Guardian*, had handed over to Alastair Hetherington in the summer of 1956 and died soon after. That was how I came to join the staff. Wadsworth, I am told, put off difficult administrative decisions as long as he could. He did not want Madeline Linford to resume her editorship of the women's page when more space became available after the end of World War II. There must have been a temperamental incompatibility, for Miss Linford's Mainly for Women was as stimulating to lively female minds as Woman's Guardian was later. 'I suppose we ought to start a women's page again,' Wadsworth is reported to have said to his then night editor, N. J. N. Dixon. 'You had better look after it for the time being.' And Dixon did, for several years, fitting it in with all his other duties, which by the time I arrived included Letters to the Editor, travel features and obituaries. (It was he who arranged the paste pot, typewriter and scissors.) He was a thorough professional and the page pottered along quite interestingly in his care, but Hetherington cannot have needed much convincing that the time had come to recruit a woman to help to run it. I sounded my friends on the *Guardian* staff and then wrote to him. He interviewed me and gave me the job without, so far as I know, interviewing any other candidate. I was on the spot, had had quite a lot of experience and was known to a number of senior people on his staff.

Norman Dixon and I scarcely met in my first two *Guardian* years, for I dashed home at 3 p.m. to be in the house before my daughter got home from school, and he did not come on duty until 4 p.m. but we had an excellent working relationship. I left everything for him to vet and he never queried my judgement about the selection of articles. Neither of us felt the other was a threat to status or an interloper and I learned much about *Guardian* ways and *Guardian* standards from him. But it would have been a lonely sort of life if it had not been for Nesta Roberts, already a friend, and then deputy news editor, who looked in for a quick gossip every morning. I had a modest confidence in my ability to do the job but no one except her with whom I could talk things over. My brilliant colleagues scared me. In the room on one side of me was Paddy Monkhouse, then deputy editor; on the other J. R. L. Anderson, an assistant editor. For months, perhaps more than a year, they scarcely spoke to me, and I was much too timid to speak to them. I had known Paddy for more than twenty years, but his head was always down when he walked the corridor. J. R. L. A. was probably as shy as I – a restless, brilliant, eccentric man who astonished me one day by asking me out to lunch and telling me a version of the story of his life. As we walked back to the office he said sadly, 'Life grows bloodier and bloodier,' but I never learned why. Thereafter he would occasionally explode into my doorway, engage me in animated conversation for ten minutes and sidle out crabwise while I was in mid-sentence. Once he dumped his red-haired baby daughter on my desk and shot out without a word.

The Old Corridor people were, except for Mary Crozier, daughter of W. P., scarcely aware of my existence. It was Mary who alerted me to the necessity of establishing my initials. 'You'll never get any proofs if you don't.' Though by my time the initials tradition of the *Guardian* was beginning to break down, it was still customary to refer to Norman Dixon as N.J.N.D., John Anderson as J.R.L.A., Paddy Monkhouse as P.J.M. Scott of course was, and still is 'C.P.' As I walked down the booklined Old Corridor to that useful place marked, like

49

all *Guardian* loos, 'Private', I might see David Marquand's long legs stretched from the bookcase on which he perched to the desk top of Harold Griffiths, economics expert, with whom he was no doubt discussing leader topics, but I never exchanged a word with David until I met him, years later, when he was an M.P., at the home of John Rosselli, another ex-*Guardian* man, in Brighton. The famous division between the Corridor (leader writers and specialists) and the Rest had relaxed, but without deliberation or intent it persisted.

So at the beginning of Alastair Hetherington's reign there was the Corridor, the Room (reporters), a vast room rather thinly-populated with sub-editors working at roll-top desks, Sport and Pictures (two photographers and an art editor). Most of the rest of the floor space was taken up by the ramifications of the library. There was no need for 'conferences' for everything could be discussed face to face or by phoning the tiny Fleet Street office. The *Manchester Guardian*'s circulation was around 150,000. I doubt if 'Features' was a word either used or comprehended in Cross Street in 1957. The sum total of what would now be called Features consisted of the 'back-pager', an essay-type article which kept its name long after it had been transferred to an inside page and through which many fine writers found their way on to the staff of the *Guardian*; 'Miscellany', a collection of oddments edited by that brilliant, sad man Gordon Phillips who wrote the witty 'Lucio' verses; 'the Miscellany Start', a two-column, often compulsively readable news-feature, contributed by reporters; 'Country Diary' and a twice-weekly half-page of articles of special interest to women. The main leader-page article, known to this day as the L.P.A., was heavily political. There was no attempt at newspaper display or design.

What Alastair Hetherington took charge of in 1956 was a views paper rather than a newspaper, revered round the world but with its heart as well as its feet, and its main circulation, in Manchester. It was international and regional but not national. It was admired in Fleet Street for the quality of its writing, respected for its political influence, but regarded as not much better than a joke so far as its news and picture service were concerned. Even in 1960 when my young daughter was looking for a job as a beginning, she was told kindly by the then women's page editor of *The Times*, 'You would do better to start on a good provincial paper like the *Guardian*.' I doubt whether even Alastair Hetherington's ambitions at the time of his appointment stretched as far as transporting his seat of power from Manchester to London. Even after London printing started he went on assuring the Manchester staff for several months that he himself did not envisage moving to London 'in the foreseeable future'. No one I knew, except perhaps Laurence Scott, C.P.'s grandson and chairman of the company, was thinking of such a startling development or would then have envisaged Alastair as the man who, on the editorial side, would accomplish it. People who knew him at the time of his appointment regarded him as able but limited; an excellent foreign editor with special knowledge of defence and strategy, with less knowledge of home politics and very little knowledge of the whole cultural field; and a bit of a stick.

I was in our bedroom when I took a phone call from my husband to tell me of Alastair's appointment as editor. I gulped, 'I'm sorry; I can't talk,' put the phone down and sobbed into the pillows. I had only met Alastair once or twice then but I knew Patrick Monkhouse and admired and respected him more than almost any journalist I had ever met – or indeed have met since. He seemed to me the quintessential *Guardian* man, in his gifts, his attitudes, and above all in his incomparable integrity. I had never accepted the possibility that anyone else might succeed Wadsworth. Because of Hetherington's stand at the time of Suez I was quickly able to tell myself, 'It's going to be all right,' for it must in a newly-appointed editor, deprived of the support of his mentor Wadsworth, have taken the degree of courage and integrity one regards as essential in a *Guardian* editor. But I went on puzzling for years over why Monkhouse had not been appointed, until one day at lunch in the *Guardian* canteen the conversation around me provided an acceptable answer. Laurence Scott, Charles Markwick, the brilliant production manager, Larry Montague (another grandson of C. P. Scott), Tom Henry, editor of the *Manchester Evening News* and Paddy Monkhouse were all about the same age, round about fifty. The trustees no doubt had it very strongly in mind that two editors in succession, W. P. Crozier and A. P. Wadsworth, had died untimely. And in fact two of the key group of men at this time, Montague and Markwick, did not survive to see the *Guardian* move to London. Hetherington was only in his mid-thirties. He had time to grow in confidence, in overall grip, even in grace. Whether he was the best choice of the men available at the time of Wadsworth's retirement no one can know. What is certain is that his mental and physical vigour was an important factor in carrying the paper through the bad years of 1965 and 1966 when a financial crisis threatened its survival. There is nothing flabby about him. There was no likelihood that he would crumple or crack under strain.

Whatever political historians may write about Alastair Hetherington's editorial policies, newspaper historians must recognize that his 'boy scout' qualities were of real value. There is no trace in him of either the mogul or the mandarin, no snobbery either social or intellectual. The youngest reporter can call him by his first name without embarrassment to either. He will not be remembered for his social graces yet it was he, with his delightful wife Miranda, who ended the division between the Intellectuals and the Rest. I can remember when Norman Shrapnel, a distinguished writing man, was asked to an editor's sherry party, but his next-door neighbour, W. E. Cockburn, who as news editor was 'faceless', was not. When the Hetheringtons give an office party at Blackheath everyone is invited, down to the newest secretary, with husbands, wives, and sometimes children too. I am certain that this breaking down of barriers has been a factor in the *Guardian*'s success. My *Guardian* work has kept me too much on the sidelines for me to judge how much today's *Guardian* is Hetherington's creation but it is strongly my impression that to an extent uncommon in the newspaper world he has been *primus inter pares*, and that partly by luck, as well as partly by good management, he has been surrounded by a team of strong, able and dedicated men and women who do not war among themselves, either to promote their own egos, their own status, their own power, or to promote different policies for the paper. The only time I sensed an anti-Alastair 'cabal' was in the bad old days of 1965 and 1966. It was inevitable – when in trouble always blame the editor – and it passed. Sometimes I think that his lack of imagination about people and human relations, which led him to make some strange appointments (not all, by any means, turned out badly) and do some very hurtful things without even suspecting they were hurtful, has had its advantages. Having so little sensitivity to personal strains and stresses he was never tugged this way and that by them. It is dangerous for an editor to become too involved with individuals.

Only the editor, the trustees and a very few other people know the whole truth of the *Guardian* financial crisis in the winter of 1966, and they will not reveal it yet. As we in Manchester saw it the threat to the survival of our newspaper came from an alarming drop in the profitability of the *Manchester Evening News*, the sister paper which was bought as a financial bolster for the *Manchester Guardian* and, hopefully, remains so. During an economic recession, advertising revenue slid away. We were confronted by a grim ultimatum that staffs must be pruned all round by one-third – which meant much more devastating cuts in the undermanned editorial section than in some mechanical departments. There were painful, forced retirements and redundancies. Promising younger men, fearing to be fired, scouted round for new jobs and got them. The bargaining between the chapel and the management which had hitherto been on an almost family basis became very hostile. There was bitter anger against 'the incompetents' who had let things come to this pass. And I swear that for many of us the anger was not so much because our jobs were threatened as that we feared that for lack of will and effort and expertise, the great *Guardian* might be allowed to cease publication. That is perhaps the supreme reason why it is the 'great' *Guardian*. Each morning as I opened the kind, anxious letters from readers I found myself wondering, 'Oh what will they do without us?'

That belief that the readers, the liberal-minded, progressive, *caring* segment of the population need a focus for their point of view is the basic reason why the *Guardian* had to go to London. From its Manchester home it could not reach enough of the people who are its natural readers. There is a *Telegraph* kind of reader and a *Guardian* kind of reader, perhaps a *Times* kind of reader too, though today's *Times* has a less positive personality than either of the other serious dailies. Not only for the *Guardian*'s sake, but for the sake of something in our democratic way of life, I hope there are enough of my kind to keep the paper going into the twenty-first century.

Well, so the *Guardian* survived, by the energy, devotion and drive of a good many people; by the strengthening of its financial arrangements; by the recruitment of Peter Gibbings as managing director, of Gerry Taylor as advertising director, and of able men on the works and management side. What I have to write of now is how the Transition *Guardian*, which I date from 1956 to 1968, hauled itself painfully out of its elitist, intellectual, semi-amateur Manchester isolation and became a tough competitor of the great *Times* and a challenge to Fleet Street in newsgathering as well as in the quality of its feature writing – without sacrificing its essential qualities of heart and mind. I can only write of the aspect in which I was involved, the development of the features section which, as I have said, scarcely existed when I joined the paper, but this section contributed very greatly to the *Guardian*'s increased circulation. In these days of instant news by television and radio, the writing man who has skill in words as well as courage and independence is by no means expendable. Intelligent readers want still to know the why and the wherefore, the 'feel' of the situation and the people who make things happen.

The founding father of the *Guardian*'s features section was Brian Redhead, a lively, perpetually youthful-looking, bouncy industrial reporter when I arrived. (He became editor of the *Manchester Evening News* and even better known for his TV appearances and his long-running Saturday night chat programme 'A Word in Edgeways'.) I don't doubt that he talked Alastair Hetherington into creating the new job of features editor; he is one of the liveliest, most persuasive talkers I have ever known, and certainly the quickest verbalizer, tossing ideas into the air, decorating and embroidering them, poking fun verging on the malicious, using an *enfant terrible* façade as cover both for a driving ambition and a basic sincerity. When Brian was appointed, in 1958, he set about building a small empire. One can see now that he was right. If the non-news aspects of the *Guardian* were to be developed, it was necessary to develop a separate ethos for features, and this Brian did, to the great gain of the paper. He inspired a strong loyalty in his staff – and a certain amount of hostility in the Manchester reporters, who felt they were being excluded from special feature writing (the coveted 'Miscellany Start', for instance), which is often the most rewarding form of writing for a reporter. One of the men he recruited was Philip Anthony Tucker, now, by one of the astonishing *Guardian* transitions which sometimes pay off, its highly regarded science correspondent, though he trained as an art student. Phil and Brian between them developed the 'wide open spaces' technique of newspaper display which made Fleet Street sit up and take notice. It was a revolution which the *Guardian* sorely needed.

The editor had made it clear to me that the women's page editor was responsible directly to him and not to the new features editor, and Brian did not interfere with my choice of material, but the time came when he took over the make-up of the page. A paper needs cohesion in its appearance as well as in its contents, but I had always very much enjoyed page make-up and the implication that I did not do it as well as it ought to be done, that I was perhaps causing difficulties in the composing room, was hard to accept. It is gratifying and consoling to me that several of the *Guardian* features make-up sub-editors are now women; I wish one of them could have been drafted to work with me in those transition days. By the time Brian Redhead left the *Guardian* to go to B.B.C. TV – though only for a year because he is, despite his charm and fluency as a public performer, essentially a newspaper man – the paper was printing in London, and the new features editor, John Rosselli, was London-based. The appointment caused some dismay in Manchester. It was, after all, a crack in the shell of the new features department, and, worse, a crack in the shell of the Manchester office, already uneasy and troubled at the increasing importance of the London end, and very dubious about its effect on the paper. None of the then features staff knew Rosselli – but I did, and I estimated him as one of the finest

54

minds and most admirable and lovable people who ever served the *Guardian*; a superb writer in whom intellect and compassion are equally matched.

John Rosselli is the son of an English Quaker mother and an Italian Jewish anti-Fascist (who, with his brother, was assassinated in the Bois de Boulogne, after the family had fled from Mussolini's dictatorship). He was reared and educated in Paris, England and America, which sounds like the forcing ground for a bitter, rootless man, but in fact, probably because of a basic sweetness of temperament, produced a man drawing strength and understanding from his roots both in Europe and America – the kind of 'man of the world' whom the world so much needs. His stint as features editor was all too short for me, for he understood and supported what I was trying to do, as an equal partner, not as a superior. He took the view that the women's page reflected a definite personality, that this was its strength, and that I should be left to get on with it in my own way. Alas, the job as Rosselli interpreted it was killing. He had a lot to learn on the technical side, he had to win the support of the features staff, and he was up and down between London and Manchester at least once a week. Alastair Hetherington, physically a much more robust man, has revealed how trying he found this pattern of life – in 1963 he spent 68 nights on the sleeper train between London and Manchester. So, very largely, I believe, for his family's sake, John Rosselli left us for Sussex University, his chief legacy to *Guardian* features being the development of articles about the arts (as distinct from notices of artistic events) which paved the way for the present Arts Guardian. But he is still stimulating lively minds. In 1969 I was on a Greyhound bus travelling from San Francisco to a remote spot in northern California and my reading was disturbed by an acrimonious argument between a young student and an arrogant hardline schoolboy. After a while the student turned round to me and apologized for the heat of the voices, and so we got talking. It turned out that though he was American, he was one of Dr Rosselli's students at Sussex. I minded less about the *Guardian*'s loss from then on.

When Rosselli departed there was no question about the next features editor being a member of the London staff, and it was Christopher Driver, whom I estimate as being, in my time, the man most like the austere, forbidding C. E. Montague – a purist and perfectionist over the written word; subtle and complex, difficult to know. For months I was disconcerted, irritated, hurt by the acidity of Driver's intellectual judgements and baffled by his long silences on the phone or even face to face. He questioned my judgement; he would not accept that my long experience of 'women's' journalism gave me any claim to respect as an 'expert' in women, he needled me about clichés. (Once I exploded, 'I'm not afraid of a good cliché if it says exactly what I mean.') He disliked any suspicion of 'cosiness' about the women's page, especially subjects like breast-feeding, and he teased me rather tartly about my apparent preference for elderly women of character over the photogenic young. During that period I needed rather a lot of propping up from K and I found myself compulsively writing and rewriting quite small items to meet Driver's exacting standard. And then, overnight, Christopher and I became friends. On K's suggestion we invited him to stay with us on one of his visits to the Manchester office. K devised a splendid dinner, and after it Christopher and I sat down to play piano duets. We both retracted our prickles and found we could make one another laugh. He had – as Nesta Roberts had predicted – done me good and sharpened my critical faculty. We are still friends.

Driver's main contributions to the features section of the *Guardian* were providing a platform for discussion of religious and philosophic ideas – too abstruse for some readers but too valuable, I thought, to be lost when he left us – and food and dining out articles. I am neither gourmet nor gourmand, but his own 'Archestratus' articles completely won me over. They seem to me still the most readable, elegant, amusing and incisive of any written about food. So Driver was a God man and a food man. Slow, oh so slow, to put his thoughts into speech and so marvellously quick and sure when shaping them on the typewriter. Did C. E. Montague write his careful prose so swiftly? I doubt it; but Montague could not have faulted Driver's grace, lucidity or economy. A women's page editor of *The Sun* once said to me, 'Everyone benefits by cutting.' Not true. A real artist, such as Driver undoubtedly is, can seldom be cut by a sentence without some damage. Typically, he left the *Guardian* to edit the *Good Food Guide* and write a book about the new universities around the world, and he was succeeded in the autumn of 1968 by Peter Preston. But at that point the new *Guardian* was struggling out of its chrysalis, and there is more to be said about the women's page of the Transition *Guardian* before I can write about the *Guardian* as I see it now.

From 1922 when she launched the *Manchester Guardian*'s women's page up to the time when the page was put into cold storage during the war years, Madeline Linford never had an editorial assistant. Neither did I, from 1957 to 1963 when the page again became daily. Public Relations Officers used to ring me up and say, 'Can you send one of your gels to our press party?', and while explaining politely that I didn't have any 'gels' I smiled contentedly. The way Miss Linford and I ran our pages wouldn't do now, but it was very satisfying and the result, in her time as well as mine, had its strength and vitality as well as its obvious weakness. Miss Linford had her 'regulars' and so had I – the only one I inherited from her was Ambrose Heath, the cookery writer. Alison Adburgham, wittiest and most elegant fashion writer of our day who became the most authoritative, and Phyllis Heathcote, our Paris fashion writer, had been recruited by A. P. Wadsworth. For the rest I backed my fancy from the unsolicited manuscripts that came in at the rate of at least fifty a week for years. I reckoned myself a *Guardian* woman through and through so that my range of interests was likely to be shared by a fair proportion of women readers.

It was so shared. The community of interest with the readers made Mainly for Women feel like a sort of club to many of them – they still tell me so – and they, the readers, were to a great extent the writers also. I think that the risk of cosiness and amateurishness was balanced by the freshness, sincerity and variety of many of the articles we carried. More sophisticated colleagues were apt to say that professional journalists also had personal experiences of value to relate and would write them more effectively, but even now I wonder whether this is quite true. The professional writes more skilfully, but the 'amateur' who has a natural gift for writing often carries more conviction. Readers often identify more closely with the non-professional, for the professional seems to them a different kind of animal, living a different kind of life, whose sincerity may seem suspect because finding subjects to write about is her job. Of course, using outside contributions to fill the women's page was a necessity when no money was made available to pay the fees of first-rate professionals, much less the salaries of staff, but virtue certainly came of this necessity. Undoubtedly the women's page of the Transition *Guardian* influenced the pattern of other serious newspapers' women's pages. Personal experience stories like that of the mother whose son became a heroin addict, the girl who described her abortion, the mother whose daughter had an illegitimate baby, the father who left his wife and family, are almost a commonplace in the 'posh papers' now, but it was *Guardian* women who opened the door to the fashion – only it is more than a fashion – of 'telling all'.

When you rely on unsolicited manuscripts the result is bound to vary in quality, but the richness of the variety must mean pleasing some of the readers some of the time; at least I often pleased myself. There was a young woman who ran a farm in Yorkshire; a housewife who had a village shop in Wales; there was Betty Thorne, living in a two-up, two-down slum house in Sheffield; and there was the idiosyncratic humour of Pippa Phemister and young Janie Preger (only sixteen when I bought her first article); there were women who had an ear for children's conversations or an eye for the countryside. And of course there was the exchange of ideas between writers and readers which I am certain was the most significant and important aspect of 'Mainly for Women' in my time. I initiated the 'opinion column' as a Monday feature labelled 'Women Talking' in 1962, and writers of the quality of Lena Jeger, M.P., Shirley Williams, M.P., Marghanita Laski, Taya Zinkin, Margaret Drabble, Gillian Tindall, contributed to it frequently. (There were no other signed opinion columns in the *Guardian* until the editor stole Lena Jeger from me when he started the back page opinion column – later taken into an inside page – perhaps I gave him the idea!)

The ideas we explored were often about women as wives, mothers, widows, workers, but were also about the whole human condition, the way we live now, the way our children will live; about relationships, morals and manners; about education and the social services and the gaps in the Welfare State. Sometimes the exploration had immediate as well as long-term value. Something I wrote stimulated Megan du Boisson and Berit Moore to suggest the formation of the Disablement Incomes Group. What Ann Armstrong wrote about her life as a 'responaut', paralysed by polio from her neck to her feet, stimulated Enid Hopper, then joint managing director of Gamages, to found the Invalids at Home Trust to raise and administer funds to help the disabled to live in their own homes rather than in hospital. When Sir Keith Joseph initiated legislation to provide a constant attendance allowance for the severely handicapped he acknowledged that this might never have happened but for Megan du Boisson and Ann Armstrong. Something Betty Jerman wrote about the narrowness of life in a new suburb stimulated Maureen Nicoll to suggest the formation of the 'Liberal Minded Housebound Housewives', which later became the Housewives Register, a lifeline for young women tied to the home by young children and starved of stimulating conversation. A letter to Mainly for Women from Belle Tutaev started off the Pre-School Playgroups Association which has done so much to fill the gap left by government refusal to spend money on nursery education. Early *Guardian* publicity helped to launch the National Council for the Single Woman and her Dependants and the National Association for the Welfare of Children in Hospital which radically changed the attitude of doctors and nurses to the presence of mothers in hospital with their sick children.

These are only the best-known of a whole range of 'do-it-yourself' organizations which have affected legislation, influenced medical and education practices, or just made life a little easier or more enjoyable for some section of the community. I would not like it to be forgotten that it was the women's page of the Transition *Guardian* that was the midwife for such as these. Perhaps it is not forgotten. Early in 1971 there was a letter on the page from a woman doctor who said that as a firm supporter of women's liberation she had always felt some guilt in turning first to the segregated Women's Guardian. When she learned from an article of mine that the women's page had been the launching pad for so many 'Women's activist groups', her doubts disappeared!

It is impossible to assess the worth of one's own contribution to any communal enterprise. I can only say that what it *felt* like to me was that I was at the centre of an operation of some value to a good many women. I had a pretty close relationship with the readers and contributors. If the readers wrote to me I wrote back. I discussed with the contributors. I talked quite a lot on public platforms, especially to women's organizations. When I retired from the staff at the end of 1971, one distinguished contributor said to me in tones of mock grief, 'What shall I do without my Mum?' I never pictured myself as a mother figure, but rather as a necessary connecting link between the paper, the writers, the readers and the activists. It was a job worth doing and I am glad I had the opportunity of doing it for the Transition *Guardian*.

The operation began gradually to change character from the time the *Guardian* opened up in London; the rate of change accelerated from the time the features editor was in London. The fact was that though Mainly for Women had the devoted loyalty of its existing readers this sort of 'club' atmosphere was not, perhaps, easily promotable among non-*Guardian* readers – and the *Guardian* was very sorely in need of increased circulation. 'Page traffic' surveys had showed that the women's page came high on the list of things readers actually read or looked at, but circulation surveys indicated that our proportion of women readers was lower than the *Telegraph*'s and *Times*'s. As the change towards a greater professionalism, a younger image, began to show, I had many reproachful letters from 'old faithfuls' to answer. It was not a very happy time, especially as there was a distressing split in thinking between the Manchester and London offices. By and large 'my' kind of women's page was approved in Manchester because of a fear that there was a will to turn the whole paper into a trendy, metropolitan affair which would lose many of the readers we had without necessarily winning the new readers we needed. Before the decision to print in London was taken, the old *Guardian* was putting on circulation at the steady rate of about 10,000 a year and was touching 200,000. There are probably still people in the Manchester office who wonder whether an increase in circulation to 350,000 justifies the vast expense of the London operation. But, of course, there can be no retreat. It was nonsense for Cecil King and Lord Thomson to tell us patronizingly that if only we would return to Manchester all would be well. The fight now is not to extend the circulation of the *Manchester Guardian* but to prove the viability of a truly national paper which is the voice of liberalism, radicalism, generosity and concern, and the fight has to be on every front, promotion, advertising, presentation, management, finance, as well as content.

Integration of effort was obviously vital and the transfer of the control of the paper to London made this more practical. I remained in Manchester – there was no question of my moving while K was alive and after his death I had a psychological need to remain in the same home – and being distant from the seat of power was probably the most important reason why my autonomy as women's page editor was eroded. I do not know whether Christopher Driver's brief from the editor specifically included control of the women's page but it seems likely. He, of course, was the spokesman for the whole features section at the editorial conferences. If there were pressures to sharpen the image of the women's page I was not there to confront them. Whether or not there was any intention to limit my autonomy it is the fact that I let authority drift out of my hands. I am not a battling woman and am very conscious that a battling woman is likely to incur more hostility than a battling man. I was within sight of retirement and was not prepared to risk being shuffled into some back alley for the last few years. Newspaper men call the obituaries file 'the coffin' and it can be a coffin in more senses than one, for many a far greater journalist than I has been deprived of executive duties in his later years and confined to this necessary, unpopular job. So I was complaisant and co-operative and there was no real need to replace me for I was useful in various ways right up to my retirement, as an organizer of the copy flow, as a contact with readers and contributors, as a writer and sounding board, and as a 'front woman' in the public eye.

But it was not until what I call the 'new' *Guardian* was born, in the autumn and winter of 1968/69, and when Peter Preston, as new features editor, was invested with full control of the two centre pages of the paper and the two preceding them, Arts and

Women's – that the extent of the male take-over was really made plain. It was not quite as hard to accept as might be thought. Preston, former education correspondent and then writer for three years of a sharp-edged, ironic Miscellany column which won him a National Press Award, is a very remarkable young man, unquestionably one of the most able I have worked with on the *Guardian* or anywhere else. I do not at all underestimate the contribution to re-vivifying the *Guardian* made by John Cole, the deputy editor, Jean Stead, news editor, Brian Jones, who took charge of the paper at night, and the quite remarkable bunch of reporters and columnists who won award after award, and lifted the news coverage to a level that Fleet Street no longer dared to talk of patronizingly. But Preston's creation was an integration of news and features, an instant flow of background explanation and comment which could have been superficial but in fact, because of the quality of the writers, scarcely ever was. The 'facing leader page', his most important contribution to the paper, revealed both his instinct for what is currently important and newsworthy and his ability to integrate. Everyone who works for the *Guardian* wants to make it a good paper; Preston, who became Editor in August 1975, aims to make it a good paper that will *sell*.

Some colleagues found Peter 'difficult' for he plays his cards close to his chest and has an odd, shy, inarticulate way of explaining what he wants. 'Y'know', 'sort of', 'as they say'. I never found any difficulty in understanding him for I watched rather than listened and a *moue* or a grin was as good as a mile of words and much quicker. When I took the week's schedule of women's page articles to him we had it all settled in minutes. 'You think that day's page is a bit lacking in glam, don't you?' 'Well, er . . . yes, a bit worthy, as they say.' So we juggled things around, and I thought that we lost some of the *involvement* of the readers in the page but fully accepted without difficulty that the task now was to offer something younger, more glamorous, more out-going, for our circulation department to promote and for our advertising department to offer as bait. We had to give them something to *sell*. So, for a start, our fashion coverage was revolutionized. Alison Adburgham, essentially a writer, a historian of manners and modes, as well as an authoritative guide on fashion, was nagged and jollied into becoming the organizer of a luscious spread of pictures of up-to-the-minute clothes, worn by lovely girls in trendy poses and available currently in the shops. The men chose the pictures – as much for the sexiness of the models, we often thought, as for the desirability of the clothes – and Alison's wordage shrank. It was and is a very expensive operation and it is comical

61

to look back on our early days together when the only fashion illustrations were what Alison managed to get free from the fashion houses.

Fashion Guardian paid off not only in increased advertising revenue but in reader interest; perhaps in circulation. In the summer of 1970 we carried a fashion questionnaire. Thousands of readers filled it in, causing chaos among our holiday-depleted staff. And those of us who still thought that *Guardian* women's page readers, so serious, so highminded and devoted to articles of social interest, would indicate that extensive fashion coverage was a waste of precious space were proved decisively wrong. A substantial majority wanted fashion at least once a week. Some wanted it every day.

Other factors in building up a younger, sharper image were the Monday comment feature by Fiona MacCarthy (one of the last of the debs) and Catherine Stott's interviews with glamorous personalities – eminently 'promotable' stuff. What we privately called 'Catherine's True Confessions' were compulsive reading, for she has an uncanny skill in drawing out people's intimate thoughts, in effacing herself and presenting a personality in rich depth. Actually it is not the most glamorous interviews I remember best. Her picture of the ageing Baroness Wootton, for example, I found unforgettably moving. When Fiona left us for the *Evening Standard* Jill Tweedie became the Monday columnist and she too attached a devoted fan club to herself and the paper. Only the *Guardian* among national newspapers could or would have given her the freedom and the support to develop, as she has, into one of the outstanding newspaper writers of the day. Her explorations of the human condition are sensitive, but often wildly funny. Her thinking about human relationships is radical, but also very tender.

Early in 1971 the Granada TV 'What the Papers Say' team gave Woman's Guardian a special award as 'one of the best general interest pages in a national newspaper', with an accolade for all our regular writers, especially Jill Tweedie, and I, as front woman, went up to the top table at the Granada lunch to collect the little plaque. It was exciting, gratifying, great fun. But it must now be obvious that there was a sting in all the adulation I was getting at this time, from fellow journalists, women's organizations, people I met at parties or meetings – my feeling of embarrassment and guilt that Woman's Guardian had come largely under the control of my men colleagues.

This self-questioning became quite painful in the months leading up to my retirement from the staff at the end of 1971. Was there something wrong with *me*, or with my view of how a woman's page should be run, or was there something wrong with the set-up which I ought to have challenged more vigorously? I still don't know, and my worst fear, that it was intended to put the administrative control of the page entirely in the hands of men, was unfounded, for within a few months Linda Christmas was appointed to take charge.

My very happy months at the *Observer* in 1974 did a lot to restore my confidence in my own judgement – and also confirmed me in several beliefs. I am as convinced as ever that women's pages are a useful and valuable part of newspapers if they provide a service and reflect women's thinking; that they create a sense of involvement in and loyalty to the paper which is an important factor in maintaining circulation; and that a woman editor is more likely than a man to be able to create this sense of involvement, because she is better able to understand what women like and need and usually has more concern to help and truly serve her readers.

The women's page under Linda Christmas became 'Miscellany' – an indication of the integrated nature of the whole of the *Guardian*'s feature pages. I believe that the integration of all sections of the newspaper (even though I have reservations about the label 'Miscellany'), opening up communications even in the physical sense, has been of very great importance to the success of the new *Guardian* – and has made far more intense demands on the staff than C. P. Scott ever imposed. In the old Cross Street days all those intellectual, individualistic introverts had their own rooms. It was the tradition that doors were left open, so that people could easily slip in and confer and discuss, but a shut door meant 'Keep out. Man at work'. Open plan working means a far higher standard of civilized behaviour, far more self-control, far more strain on nervous energy, for men and women sitting within a couple of feet of each other do not only handle copy, draw up lay-outs, make plans for the day, discuss ideas with staff or contributors on the phone and face to face, but write the smooth-flowing articles which make *Guardian* addicts say, 'How easily he/she writes.' There is never any privacy, never any quiet, and everyone can hear, or sense, what is going on all about him. Overhearing a telephone call, someone will shout a helpful bit of information across the room and lose the thread of his own sentence. Surprisingly many people can shut themselves off from this bedlam, but I never was one. Nearly all my serious writing was done at home.

By late afternoon in the features section of the *Guardian* Gray's Inn Road office the heat has built up to a suffocating level, the oxygen supply has decreased to the point where one may at best sweat, at worst feel sickly or faint. On some days there are troops of girls bringing in clothes for fashion photography and laying them on any available desk . . . a natural temptation for the women, and some of the men, to examine the garments and chat about them. Only highly civilized, tolerant and dedicated people could tolerate working conditions like these, control their irritation, ignore their fatigue and headaches. I never heard anyone say, 'Oh for God's sake shut up.' I never said it myself, but sometimes I was very near it. In fact though telephones are sometimes thrown back on the hook pretty violently and there are occasional small explosions of language which would come under B.B.C. censorship, people continue to joke with one another, toss headline puns around, and cope courteously and quite patiently with the telephone calls from outsiders. It may be the eager beaver anxious to invite the art critic to a students' exhibition in Totnes or Southwold; the writer of a Letter to the Editor three weeks ago who can't understand why it hasn't been published or why it is not immediately to hand on the sub-editor's desk; or a sad, crazy lady who is convinced that 'They' have kidnapped her child or are poisoning her water supply; or a secretary to a P.R.O. who croons, 'We sent you an invitation to our press party to launch a new iced lolly stick. Will you be coming?'; or a reader who thinks she read an item 'about three months ago' about battery-operated scissors or cut-out clothes for children or a gadget for unblocking sinks; or any one of the hundreds of good people who want to persuade you to publish yet another article about handicapped children, unmarried mothers, deserted wives, mental hospital overcrowding, language classes for immigrants, or whatever. Someone has to try to find an answer. The more successful a newspaper the more its readers make demands on the staff.

Why do *Guardian* people put up with all this? Most of them could earn more money, work less hard for it, and have less unpleasant working conditions almost anywhere else in Fleet Street – and probably get more bouquets. The real accolade at the *Guardian* is 'rather a good read', or 'quite a jolly piece'. The answer is that they feel a commitment to a newspaper which, despite the fact that the Lefties write it off as a 'lukewarm liberal rag' and the Righties as the mouthpiece of the permissive society, has a conscience, a heart, a purpose and an influence on the people of goodwill in the community who make things happen. That isn't what *Guardian* people say to one another, but it is why they are there.

5. THE OLD BLACK ART

Newspapers have been dying around me ever since I can remember. When I was still a schoolgirl the *Leicester Morning Post*, of which my father was then editor, stopped publication. The *News Chronicle* died under my husband's feet. Two newspapers and one magazine I have worked for are no more, though I was not in at the death throes. Sad about the *Westminster Gazette*, said my parents. Sad about the *Morning Post*, so well produced that my mother insisted on taking it, though its high Tory politics infuriated her. Sad about the *Daily Chronicle* which merged with the *Daily News*. By then I was working on the *Leicester Mail* and can remember some of the refugees from Fleet Street turning up there. I didn't recognize their lost look then. You have to have been bereaved yourself to recognize the face of bereavement. Artists and sculptors portray it as an anguished cry, but it has a bewildered, zombie face. I know now.

Perhaps the Rolls-Royce men, the Upper Clyde shipyard men, looked and felt like this. Perhaps so do the miners whose pit closes, and the small shopkeeper whose business is bankrupted by a supermarket chain. This can be as truly bereavement as losing a husband, wife or child. The men and women whose newspaper stops publication don't belong anywhere anymore. They are not real to themselves. The organism which nourished them has withered away. For several reasons, the death of a newspaper is particularly brutal. Journalists, though they may think of themselves as professionals, are not professionals in the sense of being *loners*. They have a sense of comradeship as strong as miners'. When in 1971 the *Daily Mail*, though keeping its title, was merged into the *Daily Sketch*, Bernard Levin described the scene when the sackings were announced: 'One man was crying: he was being kept on. One man made a shouting scene: he was being kept on. One man sat unable to take in what was happening, and insisting that there must be some mistake: he was being kept on.'

Then there is the fact that neither any political party nor Government nor the T.U.C. will lift one finger to save the threatened newspaper they may yesterday have called 'a great national institution; part of our democratic way of life'. The shipyards must be saved. The car industry must be saved. But newspapers, who can save them, and why should anyone try? When the *Sunday Citizen* was tottering towards extinction no real Labour Party or T.U.C. effort was made to save the only left-wing, democratically owned and controlled newspaper (apart from the *Morning Star*) in the country. Its editor, Bill Richardson, was made a knight in the next honours list.

Thirdly, the preparations for murdering a newspaper are always conducted in secret so that rivals will not scoop up the circulation on the day the new, merged paper appears. The knife always strikes in the dark. Levin asserted that the *Mail* and *Sketch* staffs heard of the merger from a Geneva correspondent who telephoned to commiserate. He may well be right. It was much like this when the *News Chronicle* was sold to the *Mail*. That story has often been told, and rightly, for it left the greatest gap in the range of newspapers available, a gap that has not been filled and probably never will be. It was that now despised article, a middle-of-the-road paper, for *middle* people; *middle* in their political views, their social attitudes, their tastes, their intelligence. But I must tell the story again as I saw it and suffered through my husband's experience as the *News Chronicle*'s northern editor at the time. Manchester was no 'branch office' to be lopped off to save money. It contributed a very large slice of the national circulation. It had its own full complement of journalists, and mechanical staff.

Sometime in the autumn of 1960, K had a call from his closest friend, inviting him for a drink – not in their usual haunt, nor any pub in the centre of town, but a remote spot in the suburbs. What this friend had to say was that the *News Chronicle* was being sold out to the *Mail*. They were two very brave men. One was betraying a confidence of the utmost importance because he knew he could trust his friend. The other knew that he had to carry this burden alone. For six agonizing weeks K did not even tell me. He told me only when he had been told officially, waking me when he came home in the middle of the night, desolate and distraught. There was then about a week to go, and every newspaper in the country was by then speculating about the *News Chronicle*. Every journalist was asking questions. *Guardian* colleagues, of course, were asking me, and I went on steadfastly lying, saying that, of course, the Cadburys would never give up. This was part of the bond – the success of the transfer must be safeguarded at all costs. The final purchase price may well have depended on the size of the transferred circulation. As it happened, K and I had seen it all before, when the *Daily Dispatch* was swallowed by the *News Chronicle*, only then the cloak and dagger operation had, even though we grieved for colleagues, a good deal of excitement, for we were on the 'winning' side. I doubt if there was any such hopeful excitement about the transfer of the *News Chronicle* to the *Mail*.

At last K was told by London that there would be no *News Chronicle* on the following Tuesday. He was instructed to keep this to himself, as, indeed, the information was kept secret from all the editorial staff in London. But on the Sunday morning K had a call from a colleague who said he had picked up this information from a newsagent. Was it true? Unauthorized, unsupported, K went to the office that afternoon, called the men together and told them the truth. I do not wish this to be forgotten, and I do not think it will be by any of the men who were there.

So that is how I learned about the face of bereavement, and how when the root system is chopped away the tree is likely to die – not immediately, for it sends out pathetic new shoots, but almost inevitably. As a boy on the *Northern Daily Telegraph* K had set his sights on the *News Chronicle*. He moved to the Burnley weekly newspaper because it was regarded as a better jumping-off ground for Manchester. He pestered W. H. Armitt, then the northern editor, until at last he was offered a job subbing City news and prices. It was something he knew nothing about, but he could learn – as he learned later how to make up a picture page (with instruction from me on how to measure up the pictures) when he had to fill in for the art editor at twenty-four hours' notice. As he learned later how to take charge confidently and decisively in the early hours of the morning when he was 'late sub', and everyone else had gone home. When he came back from the Navy in 1945, a first lieutenant, experienced in commanding men, he went steadily up the ladder until when, in 1958, Ralph McCarthy left Manchester to take charge of the *Star* in London, he became northern editor. Only one spur to ambition remained – a seat on the Board. He left home at 2 p.m. and returned at 2 a.m. never leaving the office for a drink or a meal. The *News Chronicle* was his life for twenty-six years. Never put your trust in newspapers or newspaper proprietors. The letter he received after the débâcle, setting out the redundancy terms, was cyclostyled, and began, 'Dear Sir or Madam'.

In his case, and he was luckier than most, redundancy pay added up to six months' salary and six months' compensation. The *News Chronicle* never had a pension scheme – though *ex gratia* pensions were always paid to senior staff, and we felt able to rely on this practice – and K's health was already too precarious for him to be admitted to the *Daily Mail*'s pension scheme where, as he said bitterly, he was 'taken over with the stock'. Colleagues at the *Mail* were as kind as only journalists know how to be, and I believe his great knowledge, especially of libel, was valuable and properly valued. But he never again set off for work gladly. His roots had been chopped away, and when a family disaster happened, his heart could not withstand the shock. He died in November, 1967. Not only that Christmas but the Christmas after, a Christmas card came for him from Lawrence Cadbury.

Pain makes one bitter and angry, and in bitterness and anger one is often unjust. Lawrence Cadbury was a financier, not a newspaper man. He was on the board of the Bank of England, and enmeshed in cocoa and chocolate interests all round the world. I believe that the son who was killed in a car crash was destined to become the 'newspaper' Cadbury. It is not hard to see how Lawrence lost heart in coping with the desperate problems of a newspaper which, change editors as he would, could not fight its way against the *Express* and the *Mail.* I think the Board tried to fend off the closure until they could be sure of a sale which would provide some sort of compensation for the staff. Only why was the end such a total fizzle? Why were the *News Chronicle* buildings, plant and sites in London and Manchester not sold for what they were worth? Why were there so few men of courage?

I often think of that dreary old converted warehouse in Derby Street, and of K wandering around it alone when it was deserted, the roar of the big machines stilled for ever, the linos silent and cold, the smell of the ink and the newsprint fading, the dust creeping over the desk he had been so proud to sit at, and over the telephones and typewriters. And of his coming home to me with two souvenirs of his twenty-six years – an *Oxford Concise Dictionary* and the *Oxford Dictionary of Quotations.*

Sometimes I think the Street of Adventure has become a track through a morass that will suck us all down, and that we are walking it blindfold, all of us, Harmsworths, Aitkens, Thomsons, Astors, Scotts, I.P.C., journalists, printers, machine minders, photo-engravers, engineers, the lot. The economics of newspaper production are lunatic, and no Government, no political party, no trade union, and least of all any newspaper readers, will face the truth that the proud fortress of the Fourth Estate has, like Venice, rested for more than a hundred years on shifting foundations which are being eroded still further by twentieth-century pollution. In the report of the Royal Commission on the Press which sat from 1947–9 there is a quotation from a letter to Queen Victoria from Lord Palmerston, dated 1861:

'The actual price at which each copy of the paper is sold barely pays the expense of paper, printing and establishment; it is indeed said that the price does not repay those expenses. The profit of the newspaper arises from the price paid for advertisements, and the greater the number of advertisements, the greater the profit. But advertisements are sent by preference to the newspaper which has the greatest circulation and that paper gets the widest circulation which is the most amusing, the most interesting, and the most instructive. A dull paper is soon left off.'

It could hardly be better said today, though the costs of producing a modern newspaper have increased enormously and the dependence on advertising revenue has likewise increased. Yet readers seem unable to grasp the fact that they get their newspapers much too cheap. A magazine woman journalist lecturing to a women's organization startled them by showing them the pages of her magazine and asking, 'How much would that cost you if you bought those blank sheets for writing paper?' This day I needed to buy some large envelopes – they were ten inches by twelve inches, not very good quality Manila. They cost three pence each – the price of a forty-page London evening newspaper. Does that make the point clear that the newspaper press as we know it would be impossible without a vast subsidy from industry and commerce in the form of advertising? Politicians orate about the importance of a 'free and independent press' and with their second breath insist that like any other undertaking it must be 'commercially viable'. The answer given to that by Tom Baistow (of the *New Statesman*) in his chapter of *The Press We Deserve* is the best I have read:

'The point that politicians and many newspapermen fail to grasp is that the press operates on a "commercial" basis which applies to no other industry; it is as if, say, motor manufacturers agreed to sell their cars at two-thirds of cost price in return for a subsidy from the oil companies anxious to stimulate petrol consumption – a subsidy that might be cut or disappear overnight in changing market conditions.'

Baistow might have gone further. Advertisers do not dictate editorial policy or content (though some of my magazine friends might dispute that) but the newspapers need their gold so badly that they are driven to set out their stall to please them.

69

What should we say if the need to sell more petrol affected the design of cars? Can anyone doubt that in the last few years of financial struggle serious newspapers have adapted their content and appearance not only to attract a bigger circulation but to attract a bigger share of advertising, particularly in the field of consumer goods. Time was when Laurence Scott, chairman of the *Guardian*, could say to me, 'Don't worry about the advertising "pull" of the women's page. The *Guardian* is not the kind of paper that can attract consumer advertising.' But now? Lord Thomson once said in jest that editorial matter was the stuff that went betweeen the advertisements. But it was not in jest that the marketing men at *The Times* circulated, I have heard, an internal memorandum recommending that 'the policy of the women's features should be to develop a market place for advertisers'. It regretted that 'at present women's features attempt to cover all women's interests' and suggested that 'editorial content should be concentrated on more commercial subjects and that women should be catered for in the pages as housewives and consumers'. That was such a crude re-writing of the recipe by which Northcliffe made a fortune that no news-paper of the standing of *The Times* could adopt it. But the attitude is there and has to be accepted. The advertisement and circulation men are fighting to keep their papers alive, too. They have to be listened to. They *are* listened to. Consider 'Look' in the *Sunday Times*. Consider 'YOU' in the *Observer*. Have they not developed 'a market place for advertisers'? Consider the greatly expanded and much 'glossier' coverage of fashion in the *Guardian*. Can anyone imagine that the wealth of information about goods to be bought is printed solely as a service to readers and never, never as advertising bait?

Older readers of the *Guardian* have quite often reproached me that we have 'changed our image' in search of circulation, as if a circulation of 350,000 were somehow less creditable than a circulation of 200,000. If they want the *Guardian* to stay alive they must understand the ground on which we fight. As Lord Palmerston said, 'advertisements are sent by preference to the newspaper which has the greatest circulation', and without advertising no conventionally produced newspaper could survive a week, even if it pruned all conceivable expenses, grasped the nettle of over-staffing and inflated overtime rates, filled the editorial columns with agency reports instead of the work of its staff reporters and specialists, for which any paper of character is bought and read. Advertising revenue we must have – and as long as it flows in, the ostrich can hide its head in the sand; the unions can disrupt or stop production to maintain their differentials; the *avant garde* of journalists can urge greater

70

'worker participation' in management and staffing. But when the economy slumps, advertising falls away – it is a 'luxury' expenditure that can be pruned – and every newspaper feels the draught and the less prosperous papers, such as the *Guardian* and *The Times*, are truly on the edge of a precipice, as was the *Guardian*, for instance, in 1965, when the advertising revenue of its 'bolster' sister paper, the *Manchester Evening News*, slipped alarmingly.

Doesn't it seem clear that if we want to keep an 'independent, commercially viable press' we have to look at both 'independence' and 'commercial viability' in a new way? The formula out of which the newspaper barons made fortunes is no longer a guarantee of 'the freedom of the press' (and what 'freedom' did Beaverbrook's *Express* provide except the freedom to propagate Beaverbrook's eccentric, and sometimes politically dangerous ideas?). Other ideas have to be looked at: the cutting of the import duties on newsprint; a newsprint subsidy; a Government Commission which would control the flow of advertising so that it was more equitably distributed between 'the leaders' in each section and the runners up; a direct Government subsidy administered by a State Commission – a method the Dutch, a notably democratic people, are trying out. If there was a will to keep newspapers alive, there would be a way. If they were regarded as an essential public service, politicians, economists, journalists, educationalists, financiers would get together and work out what methods could keep newspapers financially stable without subjecting them to political pressure.

Yet another Royal Commission on the Press was set up in 1974, but I had the pessimistic feeling that it would probably concentrate most of its attention on Press rights and duties – the conflict between freedom to investigate and publish and protection for the individual or group against invasion of privacy or damaging comment. Surely its main task should have been seen as keeping the Fourth Estate in being, to be hammered, shot at, abused, curbed, but *alive*? The hard struggle to finance the *Scottish Daily News* to replace the Glasgow-based *Scottish Daily Express* closed by the Beaverbrook Press – despite worker participation and the promise of Government aid; the frequent ominous warnings about the financial situation not only of the *Daily Express* group but other national newspapers, should surely have alerted the Royal Commission to where their main responsibility was and is?

The composition of the Commission did not give great confidence that it would be looking at new printing techniques, the amount of capital needed to replace methods of printing and production which have not been radically changed for almost a hundred years, and the need for education of both employers and employees in the necessity of introducing the new techniques, to save time, save money and save manpower so as to ensure we should continue to have newspapers as well as television and radio, to inform the public.

Of course, the problem would be much less intimidating if readers wanted newspapers enough to be prepared to pay the economic price for them. But do they? Circulations are shrinking. That this is so with the popular papers rather than the serious papers is in one sense comforting, but any price rise frightens off some readers even of the serious papers. Older friends say to me, 'I get my news from the radio and TV now. I only take a Sunday paper and a weekly periodical.' And there you have it. The mass circulation newspaper has had its heyday. The 'mass communicator' of the future is television. Quite apart from the fact that it creams off a lot of consumer advertising from newspapers and magazines, television has made newspapers superfluous except for those who *like* reading the written word; except for betting men and other sports fans; except for people looking for jobs, houses, and other 'miscellaneous wants'. Old habits die hard and a newspaper is a useful way of making commuter journeys less tedious. But ask a million people, 'Which would you rather give up, your newspaper or your television set?' and you would get almost 999,999 replies, 'The newspaper, of course.' It is bound to be so. The audio-visual image is so much more vivid than the written word.

Accustomed as I am to think that intelligent people get their ideas and their stimulus to thought largely from serious newspapers, I have had one or two nasty jolts. The first was when I took part in a symposium on the channels of communication arranged by the Mass Media committee of the National Council of Women, whose members are all active in public life. I took a great deal of trouble with my little speech, laying trails that I thought would be bound to stimulate discussion. Scarcely one person responded. One after another they rose to ask questions about, or to make criticisms of, television. It exclusively dominated their thinking. Then I was complimented in committee on appearing on the little screen in a hasty interview – on a subject on which I had written with the utmost care and thought, in my newspaper. The screened face was complimentworthy. The written word was expendable. All journalists know that their image and reputation are greatly enhanced by appearing on television, and for this reason most (not all) newspapers encourage their staffs to do so. As we can't beat the television channels we join them. So do our employers, if they get the chance of stakes in the independent companies.

Visual communication will ease us into Europe. Common

Market countries will increasingly exchange programmes in which the visual message will be so clear and potent that it will scarcely need sub-titles. Visual symbols, as in road signs, are already international. I don't think it will be very long before there will be a sort of *lingua franca* based on visuals which will enable us to travel round Europe without resort to phrase books. But 'in the beginning was the Word' – and the Word, the written word, is not superfluous yet. I am not quite so gloomy about the future as I sound. The future of newspapers almost certainly lies with smaller circulations, higher prices, less reliance on advertising and the abandonment of outdated printing techniques. There is an upsurge of new 'do-it-yourself' newspapers, news-sheets and magazines which seems to me exciting and healthy for democracy. They range from *Time Out* which is currently claiming a circulation of 50,000, through left-wing political newspapers, Liberationalist papers and news-sheets like the excellent *Women's Report* and *Shrew*, produced by Women's Liberation Workshop collectives and, in the magazine field, *Spare Rib*; to local efforts concentrating on local issues. What has made many of these small papers possible is the web-offset process. Typed on IBM typesetters, the material can be pasted up in a back kitchen or a tiny office. I have seen Lib girls doing it in Washington, and producing a lively, very nice-looking sheet with minimal outlay. *Time Out*'s initial capital was £70, the founding editor's twenty-first birthday present. Such little papers come and go. They have to be distributed as well as written and produced, and not all have enough supporters to sell or buy them. But the trend is there, and minority groups, and many of the young, who are disenchanted with the factory-made 'pop' press, are 'doing it themselves' and are prepared to pay an economic price for what they want.

I see the possibility that the great newspaper empires could disintegrate before the turn of the century – by lopping off one financially diseased sector after another. Why not drastic surgery to safeguard the profitability of the whole group, the management men and accountants who control the industry are bound to ask. IPC's ruthless pruning of its magazines shows how it could happen – and a newspaper with fewer than two million readers is, in the present economic set-up, likely to be a far greater drain on resources than any ailing magazine. It is a hard truth that dinosaurs that cannot adapt have to go.

But what survives is what is able to draw nourishment from its environment. If the new little grass-roots papers do survive, they might become more truly the Fourth Estate than the newspaper press has been for half a century.

6. BRIGHT IS THE RING OF WORDS

When I say 'writing' I usually mean writing – with an easily flowing ball-point pen, preferably on copy paper (chopped up newsprint) which is gently absorbent. So did my mother. She nagged us to bring home sheaves of the lovely stuff to cover with her curious looped writing in which the 'n's were all like 'u's and the 'm's like 'w's. I think it set the mental juices flowing, as it does with me. Young colleagues look at me with pitying amazement on seeing me actually physically writing. I don't mind. In fact I sometimes think that they might write a great deal more economically if they drafted what they have to say by hand first. It is tiresome to go back on the typewriter to obliterate a phrase or a sentence, or to alter an inappropriate word. Typewriter addicts tend to use too many words and to press on self-indulgently and uncritically, though they are not so bad in this respect as some tape-recorder practitioners who transcribe every syllable uttered by the interviewee as if it were the word of God.

So I am a writing woman. How do I write? Or, to put it more modestly and accurately, how do I try to write? Because I am a journalist my main aim is functional. The journalist's job is to communicate as clearly as possible what he has observed, found out, experienced or thought. He must see his responsibility as primarily to the reader, unlike the poet or novelist who can, if he likes, see his responsibility as primarily to himself or, if he can bear to use a word that now sounds so pretentious, to his 'art'. Surely everyone who puts pen to paper or taps the typewriter keys hopes to be read; the journalist *must* be read, or at least readable, or he is not only wasting precious column inches but creating a boring image which may damage the whole paper. 'The *Daily Blank* is so *dull*.' The journalist has to remember that the attention span of most readers, even of serious newspapers, is fairly short. Papers are read over breakfast, in the bus or train, over a mid-morning cup of coffee, after lunch or, rarely, in the evening, competing then for attention with the television set. Their active life is seldom more than a day. So you must catch the reader's attention quickly and hold it firmly. One turgid, ponderous sentence and you may have

74

lost it – the eye will have skipped to the next column. Too many of the facts so laboriously elicited and written down will produce mental constipation. Even the dutiful readers of serious newspapers – and there are many – who want to inform themselves thoroughly about subjects of importance may find their attention wandering, shake themselves, try again and then give up, saying to themselves, 'I shan't remember this tomorrow so I might as well not bother any more.'

So to be read, the journalist has to be economical of words and selective of facts. Selective? That is the stick which many serious students of affairs use to beat the newspaper press – that by selecting facts we distort the picture, sometimes deliberately. There have, it is true, been newspaper proprietors – like Lord Beaverbrook in the *Daily Express* – who tended to influence the selection of news towards his favoured policies; there have been, and probably still are, news editors who are only interested in a reporter's story if it seems to bear out his preconceived idea of what it ought to be: 'Wife Swapping in Sandville-on-Sea', 'Internal Vendetta Wrecks Humanities Board'. But the fact that selection is occasionally perverse does not mean that it can be avoided. If you had ever stood in the wire room of a newspaper office and seen the millions of words tapped out by the tape machines you would not wonder, as some guileless persons do, however newspapers fill all that space every day, but however they cope with trying to get all the available news in.

Newspapers cope by selecting what is significant. If for a moment you could think of a newspaper as a work of art the process would be easy to understand. All art depends on the selection of the significant. The greater the artist, the more certain he becomes of what *is* significant, and what will most economically and directly convey his message. The more skilful the chief sub-editor or night editor, the better his judgement will be of what is the significant news. The better the reporter, the more he can be relied on to give a balanced selection of essential facts. We are fallible human beings, of course, and Time is our whip-lashing master – but the utmost skill and sense of responsibility would not enable the journalist to communicate with all the people all the time. Einstein could by no means explain his theory of relativity to a child of ten from an educationally deprived background. Writing for a serious newspaper you can, and must, assume a fairly extensive background of common knowledge among your readers, but it is your job to assess *how* extensive, and steer a course between the ignoramuses and the specialists.

I think there is only one way of doing this – to analyse in your own mind what needs to be said until it is absolutely clear to you, and then do your damnedest to transmit what is in your mind, unblurred, to the mind of the reader. Alas, you will not always succeed. You may lack expertise, you may lack skill in thinking yourself into the response of readers, or you may use words, phrases, concepts which trail quite different associations for other people from those they trail for you. As Gillian Tindall put it, writing in the *Guardian* in June, 1969: 'I am coming to realize that when failure to make accurate contact occurs, it often stems from the train of prior associations that have attached themselves to certain subjects, or often words. Terms like "equality", "working mothers", "middle class", "Spock" or "permissive" have become so loaded with associations of previous discussions that it is difficult even to mention them without raising emotions that go far beyond the actual context.'

Nevertheless, though readers are at least as fallible in their reading as journalists are in their writing, I think the writing journalist, especially the writer of opinions, needs to know about these danger spots and to tread carefully. To stir up hostility on a matter which is quite irrelevant to your main argument can happen to the best of us, but should teach us to try to be more careful in future, for there is nothing more frustrating than to put forward a reasoned case for, say, an unsupported mothers' allowance, and to find that some chance, and quite expendable, phrase has given some readers the impression that you think the morals of working-class girls inferior to those of the middle classes. It isn't fun to bring the hornets zooming at your head, especially if you roused them quite innocently and unintentionally. (A young friend of mine had an unexpected lesson when she wrote rather censoriously about the unreliability of women employees and her secretary, who doubled as nanny, marched in, slapped the paper on the desk and said, 'So, that's what you think of me?') Sometimes the pained reaction to a chance phrase or simile has its comic side, as when a *Guardian* theatre critic compared the atmosphere of a rather boring play to 'a W.E.A. class on a wet evening in Macclesfield'. He should have known better, for he received rebukes both from the W.E.A. and from Macclesfield readers who assured him it rained less frequently there than in many other places, and what was wrong with Macclesfield anyway? But at other times the careless phrase actually causes pain and I think that though it is sometimes vital to express an honest opinion, honestly held, even though it may cause anger and recrimination, to say, 'I write what I write. If it causes pain I can't help it,' is insufferably arrogant.

There is one impossibly difficult area of total communication

– the joke. You may be able to rely on a common level of general knowledge among your readers but you can certainly never rely on a common sense of humour. Yet jokes we must have, and if we could devise a typographical symbol to indicate, 'This is a joke', it would destroy half the pleasure for those who did not need it. The moment of realization that your leg is being pulled is delicious indeed. That some other people do not realize it triples your sense of wellbeing. Two *Guardian* jokes which successfully pulled some readers' legs stay with me, and demand to be quoted. First a paragraph from John Maddox's hoax Annual Report of the British Deep Fat Frying Research Association, in 1957:

> 'Six mineral oils have been classified "unfit for frying" Four were found to corrode equipment rapidly, one gave off toxic vapours that proved fatal to frying operatives not equipped with suitable masks, and one imparted an olive green colour to all organic material (including human tissues) with which it came into contact.'

My other favourite was a letter from a women's page reader, Mrs Christine Dinsdale, part of which ran:

> 'I make everything for our simple needs, from moccasins to mutton fat candles. Contrary to popular belief these latter do not smell unduly and their light is conducive to harmony in the home. I do not see the necessity for new clothes and am still wearing the homespun cardigan and handwoven skirt in which I was married. My husband's duffle coat has been turned six times; the muffler he had when we first met is a tea-cosy and I hope soon to find a use for his balaclava. Khaki is a very versatile colour . . . My daughter, alone in a one room flat, against a hostile world, is researching into alcoholism. This necessitates her close participation in this dreadful thing, but she does not shirk her duty. Yes, I am more than satisfied with my life, and I know the heaven on earth I have created for my family is my just reward. How I wish the discontented women of your columns could know some of my joy.'

After the publication of Mrs Dinsdale's skit, my specially treasured letters were from the readers who wondered kindly and anxiously whether I realized that *my* leg had been pulled.

To emphasize the journalist's need to make instant communication with the reader is perhaps to present him as a purely utilitarian, uncreative, hack kind of writer, whereas he may be, as C. P. Scott claimed, one of the best in the world. The journalist needs other qualities than the ability to put words on paper (or over the telephone), such as curiosity about people, what they do and think, the way things happen. Some first-class newsgatherers are by no means first-class writers, but if by nature or nurture the journalist is 'a writing man' the fact that he must work within the twin disciplines of clarity and brevity makes for superb contemporary English. It is only because so much of what journalists write is ephemeral in its subject matter that even the best are seldom honoured as masters of the language – though the people who day by day read, for instance, Norman Shrapnel's parliamentary reports in the *Guardian* savour them with gratitude and delight.

What do I mean by 'a writing man'? Someone who has a feeling for the richness of our language; for whom words have a precise meaning but also a musical sound, a charisma, and a history; someone who has an ear for rhythm and pattern; who is too fastidious to dip his spoon into the stockpot of current catchphrases and slop them along his page. A real writer knows that words are both toys and precision tools. The 'new' word starts life as a shiny bright toy, becomes a useful tool and then has to be discarded by the sensitive writer, because its cutting edge has been dulled by over-use. 'Escalating' and 'grass roots' were good innovations, vivid, valid images, but they were vogue words yesterday and today are clichés. A real writing man can smell a cliché a reel of newsprint away and knows the exact moment to stop using it – if indeed he ever used it at all unless it was his own original inspiration as many of the brightest images are journalists'.

It is almost impossible to illuminate thought without the use of images and metaphors – or indeed to give that little quirk of pleasure which the unexpected turn of phrase gives – but the first-class writer does not deal in tarnished coins. He mints his own and pays them out sparingly. The elaborately contrived metaphor carried on too long is apt to end up in *Private Eye*'s 'Pseuds Corner'.

It was *Private Eye*, rather happily, which provided the occasion for the sort of quick flick of the writer's wrist, in the *Guardian*'s Miscellany column, which is the sort of thing I am talking about. When a 1967 issue of *Private Eye* carried the title 'Incorporating the Spectator', a solicitor's letter was immediately dispatched demanding an apology and withdrawal on the ground that some newsagents had assumed that this really did mean that the *Spectator* had ceased publication. Miscellany commented: 'A fleeting ha-ha sort of cod. But even the best cod has bones.'

To contrast that phrase with this paragraph from Ivor Brown's introduction to the 1956 *Bedside Guardian* is to appreciate how much writing style has changed over the years:

'If coma is all that is sought, it should be easy to find else-where the right literary, and even journalistic, sedatives. But Bedside Books are also Arm-chair and Fireside books for diurnal use, and herewith I recommend the reader to accommodate this volume to his cushioned ease of the evening if it be found too stimulant for his pillowed repose of the night.'

I was on the point of saying that the change in writing style was from Victorian Gothic to twentieth-century Functional, but the plain prose of the *Guardian* of the last few years has been lightened with what I can only call rococo:

'One might suppose, as Marketeering subsides for the moment, that our beloved leader would be urging cautious circumspection upon his trusty Foreign Secretary. But not at all. Harold, on high authority, is remarkably tranquil about George's assessment of the De Gaulle position; not a reprimand in sight. Only two Ministers currently wallow in Wilsonian ire: Roy Jenkins and Jim Callaghan. Jenkins has offended, it seems, by playing Mr Fixit over the Torrey Canyon, garnering credit which Downing St isn't sure was due. Why Jim is out of favour is being kept dark; but all may well be revealed this afternoon.'

That paragraph is also from Peter Preston's award-winning Miscellany column and it illustrates more a change in the attitudes of the *Guardian* in the second half of the century, than a change of style. C. P. Scott might not have approved, for didn't he say in his famous essay on journalism, 'It is good to be frank: it is better to be fair'? But Preston was writing for the generation whose watchword might well be, 'It is better to mock than to harangue.' Whatever the *Guardian* may have lost in the years since Scott, it has gained freedom from pomposity and punditry.

A loss that distresses, even infuriates, some readers, is the strict surveillance Scott and C. E. Montague maintained over the rules of grammar. (I do not remember Alastair Hetherington ever sending round the office the kind of note with which Scott peppered his staff, though, of course, there is an office style book for the guidance of writers, sub-editors, compositors and proof-readers.) Grammatical errors do occur in the *Guardian* and to some readers are as offensive as 'dirty words'. I think it is time we began to ask ourselves how much it really matters. I have been asking myself this question for some years, for I started off as a bit of a pedant myself. Something analytical in my cast of mind made me enjoy grammar lessons at school, the parsing, the analysis of sentence structure and so on. One of the things that most pleased me about Latin was the grammar

– knowing the right case, the right tense, the right mood. A sort of crossword mind, I suppose, with each part of speech slotting in correctly. It took me a long time to realize that grammar is a method of classification of parts of speech and word order rather than a set of rules as mandatory as the Tablets of the Law Moses brought down from Mount Sinai.

Probably what gave me the greatest shake-up was writing for the Co-operative women. My care for grammatical constructions, for subjunctives, conditionals, gerunds, relatives and agreeing participles was likely to muffle meaning for them rather than illuminate it. I had to get rid of a lot of 'whiches' and 'thats', and to write much more colloquially. I had to ignore many of the rules which we learned at school, like never beginning a sentence with 'and' or 'but' and never ending with a preposition. That a sentence must have a verb. These last seven words are a clue to the nature of grammar. They do not constitute a sentence though they are between full stops. But does it really matter whether a collection of words can be described as a sentence or not? Does it matter, either, if one splits an infinitive or uses a plural verb with a collective noun? Brought up as I was, I can't write 'to really think', even though it quite often makes for a more smoothly flowing sentence than 'really to think'. I accept, as most of us now do, 'the committee are', so why should 'these sort', now frequently used by highly respected writers and broadcasters, make me wince? It is because of my classical education that I dislike 'under the circumstances' and 'different to', but now 'different than' has found its way across the Atlantic, and there is no gainsaying that, 'It is different than I thought' flows more freely than, 'It is different from what I thought'.

The influence of Latin on our educational system has already shrunk and as fewer and fewer people (we shall probably soon accept 'less people') are conscious of the Latin roots of our language there will be much less fuss about prepositions and cases. 'Between you and I' may no longer be a shameful illiteracy. Not long ago a reader rebuked me sorrowfully for having written, 'Who did you talk to?' It so happened that I was reporting a conversation which I had had with my husband in the middle of the night when I might have been excused from remembering that the relative should have been in the accusative, but answering her plaintive cry, 'Does it really matter?' I should in any case have had to say, 'No, not really, so long as writers take care to make their meaning plain', which is as often a matter of word order as of cases and 'agreeing' subjects and verbs. 'Having climbed the hill, the beauty of the view was worth his effort', is an ugly as well as an ungrammatical sentence, but its meaning is quite clear. How about this? 'The standing orders committee met and having discussed the amendments with the proposers they were ruled out of order.' Knowledge of grammar would have prevented such a misbegotten muddle, but so would a moment's clear thought.

The real reason why I think we should not get too distraught over the breaking of grammatical rules is that they are no guarantee of clear communication with people who haven't learned them, and clear communication is one of the most urgent needs of our time. Indeed writing grammatically is no guarantee that people who *have* learned the rules can communicate clearly with one another, in every area of our communal life. We make a joke of our inability to fill in our tax return or ferret out the small print on hire purchase or package holiday agreements, but it isn't really funny. It is not at all amusing that the official handbook of the Cruse Club for widows has to say, 'A complete set of leaflets may be obtained from the local Pensions Office but help in understanding them may well be required.' If we hadn't grown up expecting official language to be difficult to follow, and other people's professional language at best jargon and at worst gobbledygook, we should realize that it is a ludicrous situation when one educated person cannot easily understand what another educated person has written for the express purpose of giving him information.

And if *we* don't understand officialese, what about the people on the wrong side of the Social Security counter? Can we really expect a labourer's widow to understand what is printed at the back of her pension book, 'This book cannot be assigned or pledged as security'? Sir Ernest Gowers' *Plain English* did much to knock the pretentious jargon out of Civil Service and businessmen's language, but we have a long way to go before we can prevent the ludicrous, pathetic, tragic misunderstandings and muddle that happen all the time in public and private transactions, in offices, courts, ministries, and town halls, as laws and regulations multiply and children leave school with small hope of working out what they mean. We all talk incessantly nowadays about the failure of communication in our complex society. Isn't it a vital need to shed our reverence for mandarin and acquire respect for demotic? By demotic I mean the way people actually talk. By mandarin I don't mean the language of the Establishment, either governmental or literary, but any system of forcing thought into a framework of complicated rules which only a minority of our people have learned. It is all too easy to assume that the use of painfully acquired rules and 'correct' phrases *must* convey the thought, when in fact it may – as with the set phrases of some trade union organizers and negotiators – completely conceal it from anyone except those trained in the same school.

Most children acquire only the vaguest comprehension of the rules of 'correct English', and so tend to be overawed by them for the rest of their life. A friend who deals with many worried people at a Citizen's Advice Bureau is apt to complain gently to me, 'Why do they always use the telephone or call in, instead of writing their complaint, so that they could have a record of it?' The answer is quite simple. Because they can make a fair shot at expressing themselves in speech, especially to a sympathetic listener, but the idea of putting pen to paper scares the pants off them. They don't know how and they are ashamed that they don't know how. In fact, if we want to communicate with all levels of the population, and want them to be able to communicate with us, we all have to learn to write much more as we talk.

And that, of course, is precisely what many of the best journalists are now doing. When you read Alistair Cooke in the *Guardian* you could hear his voice. The words flowed on to the paper just as they would flow into the microphone when he is broadcasting his 'Letter from America'. It is in this way that *Guardian* writing has changed most over the years. I believe the change has been entirely for the good, even if it has meant occasional 'sloppiness' about grammar, and I believe, too, that the cross-fertilization between broadcasting and newspapers and periodicals is one of the best things that has happened to the written language. I have no doubt at all that broadcasting influenced my own writing for the good. Some years ago I worked occasionally for Muriel Howlett who produced radio programmes for the B.B.C.'s Overseas News services. When she had read my script she would come on the phone to me in a Manchester studio and say, 'You don't need that adjective. The tone of your voice will do it.' Splendid advice. Isn't the worst thing journalists can say about a feature article, 'A bit adjectival, isn't it?' So you learn that word order, which governs emphasis, rhythm, balance, will often convey your meaning better than a clutter of adjectives.

Broadcasting, especially reading scripts now and then for B.B.C. Woman's Hour, helped me in another, perhaps surprising way – in public speaking. Ever since I rose on shaky legs to make some point at a meeting of the Leicestershire branch of the National Union of Journalists – aged about twenty-two – I have had a fearsome love–hate relationship with talking in public. This is nothing to do with 'nerves'. Almost anyone can cope with 'nerves' by doing the thing, whatever it may be, over and over again – driving a car, flying in aeroplanes, standing on platforms. Learning to speak on a platform isn't much different from learning to swim. The day comes when you find you are afloat and no longer afraid of submerging; the day comes when you know your wits will not drown in the terror of looking at that sea of expectant faces.

My trouble has not been that I cannot talk in public but that I can. I learned fairly soon that I have the kind of voice that makes people listen. It is embarrassing, but necessary, to confess that it was the sound of my own voice that gave me confidence. I might (may still) have been nervous and screwed up because the audience was very large, very distinguished, very unfamiliar or very 'dead', but when I opened my mouth out came this clear, warm, resonant sound. I could float along on it until I got a grip on what I wanted to say. A platform voice is nothing to brag about – it is a gift of nature, in my case no doubt inherited from my mother – and I had the additional advantage of having learned how to sing, to place my voice, to listen to it, so that the microphone is an artful aid, not a menace that strangely distorts what it picks up.

What an asset? Yes, but what a responsibility. On a platform I cannot help using my voice much as an actress would, but whereas she is using her voice to give magic and meaning to other people's words, I have to endure the knowledge that it is *my* words, *my* puny thoughts that are projected by this instrument I happen to have. It is heady, make no mistake about it, to stand on a platform and feel the silence, hear the laughter, sense that a catch in the voice may bring some people to the verge of tears. Once I was making a school prize-giving speech just after the assassination of Martin Luther King. It seemed to me urgent to say to those children that race hatred was an abomination, so I paraphrased Shylock's 'Hath not a Jew eyes.' The silence in the hall filled me with a kind of awe. I might have been Sybil Thorndike playing St Joan . . . but I was not. I was a humble writing woman who would much have preferred that those youngsters could have *read* my thoughts, calmly, at leisure, to think them over and make up their own minds uninfluenced by any oratorical trick. I came off the platform feeling, as I often do, drained and limp – and also feeling a need to be forgiven.

I know that Talkers are essential to the democratic process; that Churchill's oratory really did strengthen the British nation to endure the blitz; that those much more admirable people, the organizers, the patient plodders who write the letters, organize the lobbies, the demonstrations, the meetings, need to be re-fuelled now and again by the fiery-tongued ones, like David Lloyd George and Aneurin Bevan. I could not withhold my own little talent if it seemed it would help a cause about which I care. But in my growing-up years we were obsessed by fear of the irrational power of oratory, by Hitler's mesmeric control of the mob. Firmly in my mind always was, 'Oratory is the harlot of the arts.' It isn't *fair*, I said to myself, to take advantage of a gut reaction.

It was broadcasting that showed me the way to cope with my schizophrenia. Through having learned how to read a script so that it sounded more or less as if I were talking off the cuff, I learned how to read a speech on the platform. So I began to write everything I intended to say, word by word. At least then I knew I had done my best to communicate my thoughts honestly, whatever tricks my voice might play in the delivery. At least I wouldn't go home wishing I hadn't said this or forgotten to say that. But this way of going on is, of course, very time-consuming. Naturally I groan when I receive yet another invitation to speak. It is curious that though popular newspaper circulations are shrinking and television audiences vastly increasing, the appetite for the spoken word persists. Fifty years of broadcasting, a quarter of a century of television, may have closed cinemas and theatres but they have not visibly lessened the demand for speakers for luncheon clubs, guilds, institutes, societies which meet weekly, fortnightly, monthly to listen to someone talking. I suppose we ought to be glad that people still like their talking 'live'; that they enjoy the sense of participation, the stimulus, the sort of audience participation one gets in the theatre; that they are prepared to turn out on wet and wintry evenings rather than sit in the front of the Box. Or perhaps the odd thing is not that so many people are prepared to listen but that so many people are willing to talk? There are, in fact, a lot of people for whom giving talks is a pleasurable hobby or a welcome opportunity to give an airing to a bee in their bonnet. They are listened to attentively, they are treated hospitably, often lapped in flattery and gratitude – and the same talk will get the same response at any number of gatherings. Very nice for them. I wish I were like that, but a writing woman cannot write the same thing twice, and I am so far from being a real actress that I cannot *say* the same thing twice with the same amount of conviction.

It takes a lot of work, a lot of time, and goodness knows how anyone evaluates the gift of the gab, either the programme organizer or the speaker himself. It would be ludicrous for someone like me to try to evaluate it in money terms; only professional lecturers with agents can do that, and in my view even they are rather poorly paid for their skill and experience. So into the balance sheet against the cost of my time and effort

I can only put imponderables – a desire not to give offence, especially to friends and acquaintances, by seeming mean, curmudgeonly or conceited; a soupçon of self-importance if the inviters are Very Important Persons; a sense of duty if the Cause is one I care about; a desire to communicate to and with the young; and a trace of the base Old Eve in me which is gratified by flattery and admiration. It would be a shocking perversion of the truth to imply that I never enjoy myself on a platform, but I think my Non-conformist conscience would be easier if I didn't.

Now why is it, I wonder, that if anything I have *written* – and after all I had to acquire skill in writing as well as in speaking – moves or pleases people, and especially if it stirs them to do things, I glow with modest pride, and feel not a flicker of guilt?

7. PANDORA'S BOX

Until the Lady Chatterley trial in 1960 when Wayland Young spelt it out in his back page *Guardian* column I had no idea what f—— meant. It was rarely printed even in that form, even in 'advanced' novels, and no man of my acquaintance would have dreamed of saying it in my presence, least of all my husband. I was then in my fifties. When I was in my late teens I thought 'birth control' meant eugenics. I probably was pregnant myself, aged thirty-five, before I rather self-consciously used that word. Menstrual pain, however bad, was something I never discussed even with a woman friend. I must have been nineteen when my mother came upon me reading a book on sex I had borrowed from a very religious friend. She was horrified. 'I wanted it all to be a fairy story to you,' she said.

So I have travelled a very long way in my sixty-five years, and I think remembering and annotating this journey is one of the most useful things a person of my age and upbringing can do. How else can the young begin to understand how we were conditioned in childhood, and how else can we un-blinker ourselves so that we can begin to understand them? We, or most of us, were brought up not so much to conceal the body as to ignore it and its functions. We had no words we could use for puberty, pubic hair, womb, vagina, and only childish euphemisms for urination and defecation. Though I saw my younger brother in the bath and realized he was differently made from me and passed water standing, not squatting, no one gave me even a childish word to use for 'penis'. The period of the development of my bosom and pubic hair is a total blank to me, probably because the embarrassment of this unexplained phenomenon was so acute that I had to thrust it out of consciousness. The only warning I had of the onset of menstruation was my mother providing me with a dozen or so towelling diapers like a baby's napkins, a bag to stow them in, and a request to let her know when I had started to use them. No explanation; no word to use for this happening. When at our routine school medical inspection the woman doctor asked me if I had begun my periods it took me several moments to realize what she was talking about. It would not surprise me to discover that there are still some mothers as inhibited as mine was, but at least girls now can talk to one another, at least they have some kind of instruction at school, at least they can get hold of informative books.

In the long term, I have no doubt that the conspiracy of silence over sex did me most harm, but what I minded most when I was girl-turning-into-woman, and what makes me angry now, was that childbirth itself was a taboo subject. This taboo was so powerful that our classics mistress, an exceptionally good, sensitive and humorous teacher, balked at a reference to childbirth when she was reading to the sixth form from Gilbert Murray's translation of a Euripides play and substituted 'went into the temple to pray'. I know, because, blushing to the core, I was following the text. And I remember a girl becoming a tacit heroine because she guided the French mistress away from an embarrassingly gynaecological passage in one of Mme de Sevigné's letters to her daughter. I was twenty-one when my brother's wife became pregnant, and my mother whispered it to me as if it were a secret not very nice to talk about.

How could this appalling attitude to childbirth have come about? Only because of the assumption that even in wedlock children were 'conceived and begotten in sin'. The 'better to marry than burn' concept, fostered by a celibate male priesthood, only barely licensed sexual intercourse; pregnancy was the indication that sexual intercourse had taken place, therefore was to be hushed up. Only when the mother had given birth to a human soul who could be sanctified to the service of God was everything all right again. There were many nineteenth-century clerics who fulminated against the use of anaesthetics in childbirth, believing, one can only suppose, that this agony was Eve's deserved punishment for tempting all the sons of Adam.

86

'Hush hush' about childbirth persisted even into my day. There were, of course, ante-natal clinics where we went with our specimens and were jollied along by good-natured nurses and women doctors, but no one explained much about what was going to happen. The breaking of the waters took me totally by surprise. The advocates of natural childbirth believe that fear, producing tension, is the prime cause of labour pains. I do not entirely agree, but I am sure that when my daughter was making her way into the world my ignorance and loneliness made the pains far more frightening and traumatic than they need have been. Many women have told me that labour pains are quickly forgotten. I never forgot mine. It was a forceps delivery and no one even explained to me the reason why this longed-for baby, rich compensation for pain far greater than anything I had been able to imagine, was not put into my arms for more than twenty-four hours. My sister-in-law came to see us and said, 'She's a beautiful baby.' 'Is she?' I wailed, 'I haven't seen her.' I have often wondered if this tiny human creature didn't need me in the first twenty-four hours of her life as much as I needed her. Whatever we owe our children we surely owe it to them that they should be eased into the world carefully and lovingly and into welcoming arms? What kind of a start in life is it for any human creature to be born to a mother terrified, tortured or guilt-ridden? Even now there are people, and among them, sad to say, some nurses, who regard an illegitimate child as a deserved punishment for the wayward mother; who think that the sins of the *mother* should be visited on the children. What an extraordinary blockage in the thinking of otherwise quite rational people that you can 'punish' the 'sinful' mother without inflicting a much worse punishment on her totally innocent child.

Groping back again to my childhood, I think that society had become obsessed by 'dirt'. Lavatory functions were 'dirty' – is it possible that this grew upon us as cities became more congested and the need for a hygienic sewerage system became more acute? – and by transference, sex was 'dirty' too. These two aspects of our bodily functions became inextricably mixed, verbally and psychologically. Certain words were dirty. Certain jokes were dirty. Excrement is 'dirty' for a sound, instinctive reason, for untreated hygienically it is a threat to health, but semen, menstrual blood, sexual practices, whether normal or otherwise, and words to describe these functions are 'dirty' only in a metaphorical sense; only 'dirty' because that is how we think of things that come under the persisting Victorian taboo.

If only we could give up the use of the words 'dirty' and

'filthy' for sex jokes, lavatory jokes, sex words, lavatory words, and use them only for matter in the wrong place, dust and grime polluting our skin, our lungs, our clothes and our environment, it would clarify our thinking wonderfully. It is time that sensible adults realized that their moralistic attitude to 'filthy' language is the result of childhood conditioning, and is really class-based. During my time at the *Guardian*, if earnest young mothers spelt out the four-letter words they taught their children to use instead of the old euphemisms, I could count on two or three howls of protest from readers at 'the language of the gutter' appearing in print. I used to wonder why 'Disgusted' didn't ask himself, or herself, why he or she was so angry and offended by 'piss' and 'shit'. What's in a word? The result of 'spending a penny', 'going to the bathroom', being shown 'the geography of the house', 'going upstairs', still smells, whatever we call it. I think 'Disgusted' ought to realize that he was conditioned from his potty days by his mother to feel shame at these nauseating acts, especially if he did them in his nappy or knickers. And probably he was smacked or sent to bed, or regarded with shocked horror if he used the 'rude' words he had picked up from the maids, the char, or the crude little boys at school or in the back street. That's where 'the language of the gutter' comes from.

Despite the fact that in the winter of 1971 nearly 60,000 people signed a petition to Parliament protesting against the use of bad language on television, I do not believe there is such a thing as 'bad' language. Words cannot in themselves be 'bad', only the use of them, in certain times and places. Blasphemy is 'bad' (i.e. sinful) for people to whom the name of the Lord is sacred, but 'hell', 'blast' and 'damn' which were inexcusable expletives for Victorian gentlemen to use in front of Victorian ladies are common parlance now, and as religious fervour has declined, 'Good God' has become acceptable almost anywhere. 'Bloody', so gorgeously wicked when Shaw wrote *Pygmalion*, is now scarcely a 'swear' word at all. In the same way the Anglo-Saxon lavatory and sex words will gradually work themselves back into the language and lose their force as swear words. I do not think that it is at all shocking that these words will cease to shock. I rather wonder what people will do for expletives when this time comes, if there is nothing to drag up from 'the gutter', but that's a problem the richness of our language should take care of. I think it is an amusing pointer to the way in which early conditioning produces the 'shock' response, that though 'shit' still causes me faint embarrassment, my reaction to 'fuck' is perfectly cool. I only think it is often used in a lazy and a very ill-mannered way to give pseudo-emphasis. We don't cough in people's faces or spit on the pavement. Why should we feel free to litter our speech with lavatory and sex words *whatever the company*? To call a spade a spade is one thing; to insist on calling it a fucking spade implies an arrogant disregard of the feelings of other people. All the same I would like my granddaughters to grow up with straightforward words for natural functions; I would be very happy if they neither giggled nor blushed over bosoms and bottoms, penises or pubic hair; and I would think it an arrogant disregard of *their* feelings if any prudish adult censured them.

Knowing how comically naïve I must seem to many people born since the war scarcely embarrasses me at all. Because I had to fight my way from under the blanket of silence which smothered my childhood and adolescence, I think I have emerged into free air and have acquired some useful insights into the reactions of my contemporaries. I have had to question the reasons for the taboos that my parents, born in the nineteenth century, carried over into the twentieth, and have been driven to the conclusion that nearly all those reasons were bad and indefensible. It is a mystery, which only a much better social historian than I could analyse, how during the reign of Queen Victoria sex was driven right underground. It is impossible for today's young people to imagine the ridiculous lengths to which prudery was carried. My father could remember when 'legs' were 'lower limbs' and *table* legs had to be draped. The rise of Nonconformity, inheritor of the Puritan anti-sex tradition, must have been partly responsible, but I incline to the view that the major factor was the industrial revolution which established the male concept that not only their land and factories and goods and chattels, but their *women*, were property and so had to be strait-jacketed. Men could not strait-jacket their own sexual impulses, but because women were economically dependent on them, they could and did impose on them a metaphorical chastity belt, the ideal of 'purity', to ensure that no bastard would inherit their wealth. But how, we of the twentieth century ask, were women conned into such obedience, into such shame? How were they taught that ignorance was not only bliss but virtuous?

One of the most astonishing revelations of Victorian prudery comes in a letter from that heroic woman, Josephine Butler, to a friend, about the relief of being able to consult a woman, rather than a man doctor. 'O it is shame, shame! And not a few of us choose to die rather than be guilty of what we know before God is unbearable and not the will of God we should bear . . . my beloved mother had 12 children and never had a doctor near her. I followed her example and was carried safely through every confinement . . . we trust in God and if we die we do so willingly in a protest against wicked customs.' Yet Josephine Butler probably knew more about 'the facts of life' than any woman of her day. She went freely into brothels, she had prostitutes in her home, she met the full force of masculine rage during her campaign against the Contagious Diseases Acts, not only in obscene language but in physical violence. She emerged from one riot bruised, bleeding and covered in excrement. But no one, reading her letters, could suppose that prudery about sex marred her relations with her husband. It seems to have been an ideally happy marriage. Yet in defence of her 'purity', Josephine Butler would have died rather than let a male doctor see her body uncovered.

W. H. Lecky gave the game away about that metaphorical chastity belt when, in his history of European morals, he wrote his famous, or infamous, statement that the prostitute was the most efficient guardian of 'virtue', without whom the un-challenged purity of countless happy homes would be polluted. It was the 'purity' of the property-owning classes he was talking about, not the 'purity' of the lower orders, even their little children. Victorian women accepted that men had to 'sow their wild oats' because they hadn't the slightest conception of what the wild oats involved. Middle- and upper-class Victorian men seldom married before their thirties. How were they gratifyin~ their sexual impulses in their twenties? Not with their own kinc, but with the women of the 'lower classes' who, as that scarifying book *My Secret Life* by 'Walter' makes plain, were scarcely to be regarded as human beings. Men like 'Walter' paid shillings for the use of the bodies of maidservants, farm girls, seam-stresses, who could only earn pence by their 'respectable' trade. Some were not paying shillings, but guineas, for the use of the bodies of little girls. There are good people in the 1970s, like David Holbrook, who are so affronted by the commercial use of children for purposes of pornographic photography that they believe that in no century have children been so exploited by a permissive society. This is outrageously untrue. W. T. Stead's revelations in his *Maiden Tribute of Babylon* are so sickening that one hesitates to quote, and yet it seems essential, in order to make people realize that twentieth-century permissiveness has produced few horrors as terrible. Whereas even policemen hardened by years of experience could scarcely bear to listen to the tapes produced in evidence in the Moors murder case, during the reign of good Queen Victoria, cabinet ministers, judges, even a few clerics, were actually patrons of houses such as Stead described. Virgins were the thing – up to 25 guineas for a teenage virgin and up to 100 guineas for a young child. Stead said that one house specialized in the flagellation and rape of young children in soundproof rooms. Girls who tried to defend themselves were strait-jacketed and strapped to the beds. Some children were gagged with the leather thong used when soldiers were flogged. In the more expensive establishments doctors were retained to repair the little girls' lacerations so that they could be 'used' again, and if this were not possible, little children were actually thrown out, bleeding, on to the street. There does not seem much doubt that it was the fear that Stead would publish a list of names of public men participating in such abominable practices that made the then Home Secretary push through a Bill raising the age of consent. The wives of these bewhiskered, frock-coated men of repute must surely have been ignorant of what was going on – though reading George Eliot's description of Gwendolen Harleth's horror of her husband in *Daniel Deronda* one wonders whether some did not know they had married monsters – but the ignorance was elevated into a virtue of which women themselves could be proud. The mere mention of 'women of easy virtue' sullied them. Even such a level-headed, well-balanced woman as the suffrage pioneer Millicent Garrett Fawcett refused to ally herself with Josephine Butler's crusade against licensed prostitution because to do so might damage her own crusade for the vote. The hypocrisy of the Victorian male sickens me; the complacency of the sheltered Victorian lady sickens me almost more. When Gladstone spoke of his fear that women entering public life would be invited to 'trespass upon the delicacy, the purity, the refinement, the elevation of their own nature which are the present source of their power' no doubt many Mammas, from Queen Victoria downwards, preened themselves, for had they not been taught that it was the divinely ordained *duty* of a woman to be delicate, pure and refined and to close her mind to the thought that the skivvies, the streetwalkers, the female creatures who crawled on their bellies in the mines or sweated sixteen hours a day in the mills, were women too.

Among my treasures is a printed copy of a speech made by one Mr Justice Beaman in Bombay in 1908. It is hard to think that anyone took him seriously when he said this: 'If we could not have our fairest ladies flaunting on the platform, scrambling for parliamentary power, elbowing men in the counting house, the field of sport, and the market place, as little would we have them for ever begrimed with the sordidness of the kitchen. The frail, delicate charm of woman, subtle as the perfume of the cuckoo flower, cannot endure to be perpetually soused in the reek of baked meats, any more than the rarer beauties of her soul can hope to blossom fully and perfectly in such gross environment. We do not want the fairy queens of our gardens to be amazons and gladiators, neither do we want them to be cooks and kitchen maids.' Judge Beaman cannot possibly have been implying that *men* should take on the smelly jobs of cooking and cleaning; he must have been assuming the existence of sufficient numbers of sub-human female creatures. 'Walter' and his like made similar assumptions about the supply of female creatures to satisfy other appetites. I don't think any of the assumptions of our 'permissive' society are more revolting than that.

What has been happening in the last twenty or thirty years is that the lid of Pandora's box has been raised, not suddenly, but little by little, releasing many of the ugly things which are thought to be 'polluting' our society. Perhaps my own story of the release from needless shame about the body and its functions explains my belief in the sanitizing effect of light and air. I sincerely believe that the ugly things are less fearsome now they can be talked about than when they were festering in the dark. Larry Adler, in a letter to the *Guardian* in August, 1971, gave a telling example of the effect of a conspiracy of silence, quoting Senator McNaboe speaking against a Bill to provide education on the prevention of venereal disease. Never in his life, hoped the senator, would the word 'syphilis' sully the lips or minds of New York matrons or maidens. 'You could catch it but you mustn't say it,' commented Adler.

Ah, but how does the spread of venereal diseases look in the clear light of day? Pretty horrifying, at first glance. Gonorrhoea has reached epidemic proportions, at the rate of about 50,000 new cases a year – and tracing contacts is often impossible because the people infected do not even know the names and addresses of the partners with whom they have had intercourse. But perhaps our horror at this mindless promiscuity and our half-knowledge of the terrible effects of untreated syphilis tend to cloud rational thinking? It seems to me a great gain that because syphilis can both be named and simply treated, a genius of the quality of Hugo Wolf the composer is now unlikely to die in a madhouse while still quite young – or any other young man with half a useful life to live. If fear of a dreadful, paralysing illness had been an effective sanction against casual intercourse for virile young men in the heat of excitement, the venereal diseases would not have spread throughout the world, throughout the centuries. Is there not more hope now that they may be eradicated by a combination of medical science and education? Lung cancer is a much more dread disease than gonorrhoea but it is proving very difficult to *frighten* people out of their addiction to cigarette smoking. Yet the social attitude towards cigarette smoking is beginning to change. Future historians may see it as a curious aberration of the twentieth century, at least as odd as the taking of snuff seems to us.

So, some day, may our present monstrous preoccupation with sex seem an aberration, which was more or less inevitable when the lid of Pandora's box was lifted. The shackles of shame over the sex urge had to be broken; the Victorian dichotomy between 'love', divine and ennobling, and 'sex', 'animal' and degrading, had to be ended. The twentieth century has, some-what painfully, come to accept that the sex urge is a natural *human* attribute which enriches life, but this change has come about largely because 'sex' has come to be equated with 'love'. Perhaps this was a historical necessity; perhaps the only way to dignify 'the act of love' was to give it the full romantic treat-ment. That 'pure' wives are no longer expected to 'submit' to a sex act in which there could not possibly be any joy for them is a great gain. But when we use 'making love' as a synonym for copulation, for instant sex, we are using a euphemism as hypo-critical and, to me, as nauseating as any the Victorians in-vented. Until we shed this false romanticism about love we shall not get very far in clarifying our thinking about sex. Can a drunk and a drab copulating in a back alley, by any stretch of the imagination, be said to be engaged in 'the act of love'? The coupling of men and women is the satisfaction of an appetite; it may give great physical joy as well as excitement between well-mated partners even if they have no deep commitment to one another; it may be one of life's most ecstatic experiences for two human beings who dearly love one another, but even in its highest form it is not *synonymous* with *love* – it is only an aspect of love.

The equation: love (the highest good) = sex (the only valid expression of love) has so misled our young that one can see manifestations of synthetic love everywhere. Look at all the young people who drape themselves around each other in public places, even on commuter stations at nine o'clock in the morning. You can perfectly well tell which are the couples who are drowned in love and can hardly bear to tear themselves apart and which are the ones who are having a bit of a fondle to pass the time until the train comes in, as they might have a cigarette or a cup of coffee. No harm? No harm, I suppose, unless they kid themselves that this is 'love'; no harm unless one of the pair happens to be really painfully in love and not the other; unless one of the pair is unbearably stimulated while the other is only mildly titillated. It takes two to copulate, two to perform the sex act to give mutual pleasure, two to experience the act of love, and both are human beings with the capacity to feel, to think, to care, to suffer. The dogma which the 'permissive society' offers its young, that the sex act is natural, therefore good, is a syllogism which a moment's rational thought would destroy. A schoolgirl writing in the *Schoolkids Oz* put forward the idea that as animals copulated freely in the street human beings should have the same right if they wished it. What is natural is good? Would the poor child accept that because it was 'natural' for an oversexed man to be inflamed with lust by her nubile charms that it was his right to force her into the back of his car and rape her? Of course not, because though she has been taught, or taught herself, to think that, in her words, 'the act of making love is beautiful and natural and should be admired', she has excluded the idea of rape. Hence the need for honesty of thinking about what we mean by 'the act of love'. What can be simulated, or even, God help us, performed in public, is the sex act. Love, the total commitment of one partner to the other, is almost by definition an essentially private thing, more private even than childbirth, more private even than death.

So we have a society in which even some educators of integrity (including mothers) are at one with advanced novelists, some film-makers, some pop singers, and some writers of advertisements, in projecting love (i.e. sex) as a Good Thing, and ignoring the possibility that it can also be a very Bad Thing, hurtful, painful, disruptive, cruel. Loveless sex to satisfy curiosity is not a good thing, enforced sex (rape) is not a good thing, procreation without intention is not a good thing. Can it be outmoded prudery that makes me want our children to be spared incitement to sex experience almost from the start of puberty? Or is it commonsense and concern for these immature boys and girls and for the babies their sex experiments – apparently sanctioned by the pop theme-song 'All I want is Love' – bring into the world? Is life really less free of tension, misery and despair for adolescents now, when they are confronted by the decision, in their own brutal language, 'to fuck or not to fuck' than it was for adolescents in my day when sexual intercourse was quite outside our comprehension?

Do I put myself beyond the pale when I say I hate the adjective 'sexy'? It makes me shiver when I see a little girl not yet in her teens preen herself in her new dress, her new lipstick and touch of eyeshadow, and hear her ask, 'Do I look sexy?' She, of course, uses it as a synonym for pretty – but in fact she probably does look sexy, sexually attractive to the male. Can this really be the image that her parents want the little girl to have of herself? Do they really accept that as sex is Natural and

94

therefore Good, the little girl should learn at an early age to set out her stall to attract it? I realize that, being a woman, I am much more acutely aware of the dangers of 'free sex' to girls and women than to boys and men. But it is a biological fact that though women can seduce, provoke and sexually humiliate men, they cannot rape them – or make them pregnant. Women are at the receiving end of the thrusting penis. It surprises many men – though it really should not – that penis resentment is much more common than the classic Freudian penis envy. How many girls and women have said, throughout the ages, 'You only want me for one thing'? And how many men have laughed off the pathetic little protest, confident that as they gained pleasure they must surely be giving it? And no doubt they very often were, and no doubt many of the girls were flattered and grateful to have aroused such devoted and passionate desire – and yet still felt an inarticulate rebellion at being the object, the gratification of the desire rather than a full partner in it. Today the rebellion is no longer a feeble cry. It is fiercely articulate – which disturbs and displeases all the nice women as well as all the nice men whose sexual relations are based on mutual tenderness. Isn't it a bad case of arguing from the particular to the general to assert that Man treats Woman as a sex object, except in the obvious and inevitable physical sense of the man giving, the woman receiving? It may be; but I see no reason to run away from all the evidence which our permissive society has enabled to be published that a typical, if not *the* typical, male sex fantasy is based on humiliating, degrading and physically abusing the female needed for the completion of the sex act. It was a man, Clive James, reviewing Kate Millett's *Sexual Politics* in a Sunday newspaper, who remarked that the 'heroes' of Henry Miller's and Norman Mailer's novels seemed 'hell bent on using women as ashtrays, urinals, punching bags and stuffed sacks for bayonet practice'.

Nauseating reading though it is, it seems necessary to quote an example of what Clive James was talking about. This is from Henry Miller's *Black Spring*. (Worse is quoted, in *Sexual Politics*, from Mailer's *The American Dream*.)

' . . . "now I'm going to warm you up a bit." With that he up and ties her to the bedstead, gags her and then goes for the razor strop. On the way to the bathroom he grabs a bottle of mustard from the kitchen. He comes back with the razor strop and he belts the piss out of her. And after that he rubs the mustard into the raw welts. "That ought to keep you warm for tonight", he says. And so saying he makes her bend over and spread her legs apart.'

'*Oh, that's only fantasy.*' Well, for goodness sake, one hopes so. If Miller, Mailer and Co. really behaved like that it would surely be no wonder that poor Valerie Solanas wrote her 'Society for Cutting Up Men' manifesto and drew a gun on Andy Warhol. But accepting the fact that such sick-making distortions of the sex act as the one I quoted are peculiar to a very few, sexually abnormal, exhibitionist writers, there are still questions we should put to the men we like, love and marry, pressing them for answers. There is no doubt that rape is very much on the increase, and has become so frequent in the United States that women have set up 'rape crisis centers'. Why has this happened? Young rapists who have been willing to talk have indicated that they felt a compulsion to justify their virility – and to establish it in the eyes of their peers. It is not true that all rapists are mentally disturbed. Equally it is certainly not true that all women who have been raped have invited it, by their dress, by their manner or even, if you please, by their *fear*, which has been said to excite men as an old lady's fear excites the dog yapping at her heels. Girls of my generation were always warned that men found it much more difficult than women to control their sexual impulses and that we must beware of exciting them beyond the point of no return. It might be a good thing if that were still dinned into girls' heads – though it doesn't seem very complimentary to men, and girls do not often feel now that their virginity is priceless – but nothing in a girl's dress, manner or behaviour can protect her against the stranger who attacks her in a dark alley or breaks into her flat.

Do most men believe that every man is a potential rapist? Surely not. Do they believe then that sadistic rape fantasies are buried deep in the dark subconscious of normal men and the Miller/Mailer fantasizing is cathartic? If so, can they understand that what they expose in their writing may be as offensive to a woman as spitting in her face or urinating in her sitting-room? And if they can understand this, how is it that they write off Valerie Solanas's fantasies as the product of a diseased mind but laud Mailer, Miller and their like not only for the quality of their writing but for their honesty in revealing the murky depths of human behaviour, and would almost go to the stake for their right to publish what to this woman's mind is sadistic pornography?

To draft a legal definition of pornography or obscenity is practically impossible, if only because the level of tolerance differs from generation to generation, from culture to culture, even within our own country, our own age. There are people who think that any representation of the naked human body is

obscene, and many more who think that any explicit representation of either male or female private parts is obscene; a very
great many more who think any representation of the sex act
obscene or, indeed, pornographic. I think this kind of factual
material will, and should, gradually work itself into public
acceptance and would accept the risk of its over-exciting some
'voyeurs' for the sake of spreading greater understanding of how
our bodies are made and how they function, so long as it is not
thrust upon children who have not been prepared, at home or at
school, to accept it without prurience or fear.

My own subjective definition of pornography would be anything that deliberately *uglifies* sex, especially by exaggerating its
trace element of sado-masochism. Even if one can accept a
very wide range of sexual behaviour between consenting adults
as 'natural' therefore 'good', it does not seem to me that a
civilized society should accept within this definition bestiality,
sadistic violence or the exploitation of children. Indeed, hardly
any of the 'Permissives' would disagree; but what some would
say is that since these aberrations exist they should be discussed
openly rather than concealed. Right, if they are discussed in
psychiatrists' case histories; wrong, if they are fodder for porn
merchants to sell to all and sundry, including the mentally and
sexually unstable; a thousand times wrong, if they are put before
adolescents as exciting ways to shock their elders; a million
times wrong, if they are put before young children to whom the
sex act is still rather a frightening mystery.

Even if all children today were brought up to accept their
bodies without embarrassment and to understand the facts of
sex from the earliest age – and they are not – the gross distortions of the sex organs which appeared in underground publications like *Oz* seem to me more likely to terrify an innocent
child (using 'innocent' in its precise, not sentimental, sense)
than to corrupt it. It surprises me that the whole of the long *Oz*
trial was devoted to considering the possible corruption of the
adolescent, and that no one, so far as I know, considered the
offence against the child.

And so what about censorship? It is one of the most difficult
moral questions of our time and I don't think any thoughtful
person should avoid questioning himself very searchingly on
where he would draw a line, if at all. I think we have to walk a
tight-rope all the time between freedom and protection of the
vulnerable. The most vulnerable are children who may be
frightened by nightmarish representations of what they cannot
understand, or coarsened by encouraging them to accept that
the sex act is the same thing as the act of love, or brutalized by
accustoming them to violence (and, of course, I don't only

mean sexual violence). It is self deception to say that parents can protect their children by censoring what they read and see. From the age at which children can buy or borrow their own reading matter parents neither can nor should attempt to censor it – the one certain way to make a child read something is to say 'you mustn't'. Society protects children against assault on the body (though not small boys against caning by their teachers). It is obviously much more difficult to protect them against assault on the mind, but I cannot understand how people of conscience and goodwill can deny that the offence exists or can shrug it off. It seems that 'moral indignation' is only respectable now on behalf of 'freedom' not on behalf of the casualties of freedom. What about the 'moral pollution' campaign then? What a very sad thing to have chosen a slogan that revives the association of 'sex' and 'filth', and so attracts the censorious, the blinkered, the repressed, the intolerant, the prurient, the fanatical, and tends to alienate people loth to be seen in such company. Best to accept that in the present climate of opinion a 'morality campaign' is likely to do as much harm as good. But to refuse to say, '*You* must not', doesn't let us off the hook of saying, '*I* must not'. And if any of us, writers, editors, publishers, film-makers, accepts a responsibility towards the vulnerable, the children, the young adolescents, the blacks, the Jews, the unstable, it is cowardly not to stand up and be counted, for fear of being called corny, fuddy-duddy, anti-freedom or even anti-life; cowardly to take refuge in the difficulty of defining what is harmful; what perhaps ought to be banned. I was quoted approvingly in the Longford report on pornography because I had written in the *Guardian* about my visit to Lord Longford's office to see for myself what his collection of pornographic material added up to. Not quite fairly quoted, I thought, because there was a lot, as I said, of material I found somewhat distasteful, probably because of my age and conditioning, and not much that I found truly 'hard porn' and was appalled by. But I *was* shocked and distressed by that smallish section, and it did confirm my belief that some strictly limited form of censorship has to be maintained. I will not accept that copulation with animals should be portrayed; that young children should be photographed to titillate the sexual appetite or fantasies of adults or that *sadistic* pornography can ever be justified, for it incites the humiliation and rape not only of women's bodies but of their integrity and dignity as human beings. However difficult to devise a 'protective' rather than moralistic censorship, we should go on trying. What needs to be done should never be thought to be impossible.

I know very well that pioneers whose names have later come

to be honoured have been banned by the censor. Marie Stopes was accused of encouraging girls to take up prostitution. *Mrs Warren's Profession* was banned. Radclyffe Hall's novel about Lesbianism, *The Well of Loneliness*, was banned. In every generation brave pioneers move us a step forward to accepting new concepts of what is permissible in human relationships. In retrospect we honour them – but it is right that they should have to fight their way in, for only by public discussion can public awareness, public acceptance, grow. I am glad that I have been forced to accept that pre-marital contraceptive advice is a safeguard against both the procreation of unwanted babies and against sexual incompatibility in marriage; glad that homosexuality has been freed from legal persecution and social horror and is beginning to be accepted as a valid form of love; glad that legal abortion has become available as a last resort against bringing into the world a possibly deformed child, a resented child, a child who is the result of rape: glad, glad, glad, that sexuality and procreation can be discussed openly and honestly.

Perhaps we should have more faith that the great current ferment over sexual behaviour will work itself out within a generation or less, and that we shall reach a tranquil acceptance. There is one factor that I have not seen discussed – the physiological function of the sex urge is to reproduce the species, just as the function of the appetite for food and drink is to ensure the survival of the individual. If the human race survives into the twenty-first century, if there is no annihilation by nuclear bombs, and if we solve the terrifying problem of overpopulation by voluntary limitation of conception, is it not possible that the sex urge may begin to diminish? This is very hard to envisage now, but *homo sapiens'* progress has been towards not only the control of his environment but the control of his own physiology. There is no doubt that we are on the way towards fool-proof, completely safe contraception (probably post-coital contraception). It is probable, to my regret and to the regret of all women who have had delight and fulfilment in suckling their babies, that breast-feeding seems to be on the decline. Especially in the U.S.A., artificial insemination is already with us, so is sterilization, of both male and female. The test-tube baby, gestated outside the womb, is certainly a possibility, perhaps a probability. How will the sex urge begin to look in the twenty-first century?

Once we have accepted that fewer babies are needed to replenish the earth, how will non-productive relationships begin to look? Probably no longer 'selfish' but admirable, if the parties lead useful lives in other ways than child-rearing; not 'perverted' if the couple are of the same sex, for the 'sinfulness' of homosexuality was based on the belief that the only justification for sexual intercourse was procreation.

And if the biological necessity for this powerful appetite shrinks, as it seems inevitable, will the appetite also decline? How is *la différence* going to look in the twenty-second century? I wish I could be around to see.

8.   LET MY PEOPLE GO

I was sitting in the Serjeant-at-Arms gallery in the House of Commons on 28th January 1972, listening to the abortive attempt to get a second reading of the Anti-Discrimination Bill; restless, impatient with waffle, wishing I had the chance to present this case myself, when Shirley Williams came to the dispatch box. As her clear, warm voice rang out I thought, 'This is it. This is *it*. This woman's fine mind, her beautiful command of words, her lucidity, her rational analysis of the situation, is exactly why I am a feminist; why I can't bear women to be talked down, to be patronized, to be pushed into a supportive role, to be denied the full exercise of their powers'. Behind me in the Strangers Gallery, where in the first decade or so of this century the Suffragettes had sat behind a grille, sat row upon row of women, mostly quite young, and excitement surged up in me, and a great sense of involvement. 'These are my people.' And then – inevitably, since what I have sung so often expresses my mood – came to mind that most powerful cry from all Negro songs: 'Let my people go.'

For most of the girls in the gallery the way the debate was talked out meant bewildered frustration, but not for me. Seeing and hearing the explosion of anger on the floor of the House, the commitment to the cause by men as well as women, Conservative women as well as Socialist, I *knew* with startled joy, for the first time, that some day, after however much more boring, trudging persistence, however many demos, lobbies and meetings, this Bill or something like it would become law; that this day was a turning point; that some day soon (in terms of my longish life) we should realize that it is *silly* as well as unjust, to prevent women from being stockbrokers, racehorse trainers, proof-readers, typesetters, bus drivers, airline pilots,

100

ministers of religion, television news readers, if they have a mind to and are able and willing to learn how. I thought of the National Graphical Association being compelled to take in women members, and I chortled in my joy. This euphoria lasted all of thirty-six hours and kept me warm as I forced my way, as I went about my domestic affairs, through a bitter north-east wind.

Euphoria is comic to those who see no occasion for it. Women's Liberation is comic, if not repulsive, to a great many nice, well-intentioned women as well as men. So one has to try to explain the what and the why; to dig down with the care, the honesty, the discipline of the archaeologist through layer upon layer of history, one's own history, as well as that of *homo sapiens.* How have women come to be, how have they come to accept being, the Second Sex? Why should I, timid youngest child that I was, have come so early to identify myself with women's struggle for fully adult status? Why should I have this basic certainty that though how I do things may be conditioned by my sex, what I have been able to acquire the skill to do has, over wide areas, little or nothing to do with having been born female? To dispose of the personal history first: I was not less able than my brothers, nor was I thought by the family to be so. My mother called herself an anti-suffragette, but her life, what she did, not what she said, set a pattern for me. She had her little newspaper job, she took the chair at meetings, she organized, she managed, she was herself, whether as wife or as mother, not anyone's appendage. I would be Me. This was, of course, all inchoate – until in my early twenties I read Ray Strachey's *The Cause.* Ah, then I caught fire; then I recognized myself as a feminist; then I found heroines who have stayed with me all my life. Here are some of them: Mary Wollstonecraft who gave us our banner line in her *Vindication of the Rights of Women,* published in 1792: 'The first object of laudable ambition is to obtain a character as a human being, regardless of sex.' Caroline Norton, fighting her abominable husband for the custody of their two children and writing, 'My husband has a legal lien (as he has publicly proved) on the copyright of my works. Let him claim the copyright of THIS.' Florence Nightingale, one of the great minds of the nineteenth century, fighting her way out of the prison of young ladyhood, 'O weary days, O evenings that never seem to end! For how many years have I watched that drawing room clock and thought it would never reach the ten.' Sophia Jex-Blake fighting for a medical education at Edinburgh against the hostility of loutish male students who delighted to cat-call the girls with foul abuse couched in medical terms which the police would not understand. Millicent Garrett Fawcett beavering away through parliamentary channels, meetings and lobbies for fifty years. Josephine Butler risking life and limb as well as reputation, to protect the women of the underworld. The brilliant Pankhursts, Emmeline, Christabel and Sylvia with their army of thousands of well-brought-up ladies nerving themselves to march, to throw stones through plate-glass windows, to chain themselves to railings, to go to prison, go on hunger strike and endure the barbarous cruelty of forcible feeding. You would think the Negroes would understand this struggle for adulthood, but it was Stokely Carmichael who said, 'The place of women is prone.'

From the rubble of the millions of words I have read and written about the condition and the nature of women, how can I claw out a few shards, a few coins of what I believe to be significant truth? The task is daunting, but one must try.

When the species (singular or plural) who evolved into *homo sapiens* hauled themselves on to their feet, biological necessity divided the male from the female. Even without a cunning brain the naked ape could not have survived as a species if he had not had a powerful, continuing sexual appetite which ensured that he would replace himself in sufficient numbers. The female was for reproduction, the male for hunting for food and for protection against attack. During the long march to civilization the male role has been sub-divided again and again, but the female role of bearing and nurturing children continued to be necessary for the survival of the species almost up to our own times. Now even though the risk of population loss from natural disasters, including plague and famine, persists and the shadow of nuclear war is a menacing question mark over the survival of man, conveyor belt reproduction is no longer a biological necessity, and indeed is now seen as a threat to, rather than an insurance of, the race's survival.

Now the quintessential inevitable division of male/female roles has so shrunk that re-thinking is imperative. Today the only thing a man can do which no woman can do is to impregnate a woman. The only thing a woman can do which no man can do is to conceive, gestate and suckle a child – and this she cannot do for all her span of life and should not, many people would say, for all her fertile cycle. So to maintain the whole structure, the whole ethos, the whole mores of a civilized society on the hunter/child-bearer polarity is as unrealistic as to go on building every home with hearths and chimneys as if the only fuel still available were raw coal. It no longer makes sense. 'You can't get away from biology' is a non-argument. Mankind's ascent from his original state has included a progressive increase in control of his physiological needs, demands and behaviour. As the functional differences between men and women lessen, as the female role subdivides, so, I believe, will behavioural differences lessen. They have, of course, already lessened very considerably, since the advance of technology, since the introduction of universal education for both sexes, since the availability of reliable contraceptive techniques.

It is easy for a woman like me, widowed and past child-bearing age, to see that whatever life on this planet is about, whatever the purpose, if any, of our being here, our function, whether we are male or female, is not simply to reproduce ourselves with worthy successors. It is less easy for the women still pre-occupied with child-bearing and rearing to see this. But when such women ask, as they often do, 'What better thing can a woman do than rear stable, well-adjusted children?', the answer seems to me painfully obvious, 'Save *thousands* of lives', as did Florence Nightingale, who never had husband or child of her own. Before child-bearing and for long years after child-bearing and rearing, even childless, husbandless, one may have immensely valuable functions which are nothing at all to do with one's female body.

Of course I have simplified the argument from biology. If it is true that the sex of a person is attested by every cell in his/her body, not just by the possession of the complementary penis or womb, maleness, femaleness, may be an essential aspect of the psyche. *But we do not know.* We have no justification for saying, here and now, that it must be so. We do not know if Mind has a sex. Whatever Mind may be, whatever the psyche may be, it is obvious that we have genes from both parents and that we inherit from either parent not only noses, eye colour, height, shapes of hands and feet, but temperament and aptitudes. If an aptitude for music (which is a very clearly identifiable aptitude) appears to have been inherited through the father's line, is it, can it be, 'feminized' when it appears in a daughter rather than a son? Some men may say 'Yes. Women may be superb executants of music written by men, but they do not create great music. Their creative role is in bearing children.' I believe that time, the necessity for women to find another role than the maternal and supportive, the freeing of women from economic and emotional dependence, will prove them wrong.

There is no lingering shadow of doubt in my mind that human beings treated differently will respond differently; that the way we treat girls from birth and the expectations we have of them, condition their responses and their own view of their life role, their possibilities; that we are all habituated to think that dolls and nurses' outfits and cooking sets are 'right' for girls and miniature cars, toy pistols and footballs are 'right' for boys. But how different are the girl babies and boy babies when they come into the world? That's a thing we don't know much about yet. My mother, with two sons before me, thought I was 'different'. Having only one daughter and two granddaughters I have not been able to observe closely for myself, but I have recollections of nephews and great nephews stomping along and shouting with a *boy* sound. Lois Mitchison, exploring illuminatingly some of these apparently inborn sex differences in a *Guardian* article in 1964, described her little daughters' endless preoccupation with their doll family, though they had been given miniature cars, tool benches and the like. Her nephews, on the other hand, said 'Vroom vroom' (the international boy babies' car sound) before they could talk, and were much more inclined to play 'bang bang' games with toy guns. A primary school teacher once sent me a selection of very young children's drawings. Nearly all the girls' were of houses and domestic cheer; nearly all the boys' were of battles by land, sea and air. But such evidence as we have about inborn differences is minuscule. We shall know precious little about innate differences until a serious effort to end sex-role conditioning, such as the Swedes are attempting, has been in operation for a generation or more. Or as John Stuart Mill wrote: 'I deny that anyone knows, or can know, the nature of the two sexes, as long as they have only been seen in their present relation to one another.'

What we do know, through the work of historians and anthropologists, is that though daily tasks have been divided by sex in almost every society since recorded history began, the division has varied from culture to culture. It is not true that basic physique divided men into hewers of wood and women into drawers of water. Ester Boserup in *Women's Role in Economic Development* says, for instance: 'To most Hindus and Arabs the idea of female participation in trade is an abomination', whereas among Africans and most people in south-east Asia a large share of most trading, selling and buying is left entirely to women. A Vietnamese man, asserts Miss Boserup, regards trading as debasing for a man, and his womenfolk are also load carriers and dock labourers. A Philippine man regards himself as being too sensitive for the coarse language and aggressive behaviour necessary in a good tradesman. In Malaya, Chinese women do the unskilled work in the building trade, such as earthmoving and foundation digging. People who thought they had destroyed the argument for anti-discrimination legislation by saying, 'What about coal mining? What about labouring on a building site?' should read Miss Boserup. What is 'women's work' depends on the expectations of the society which conditions them. Not only in the underdeveloped countries but, for instance, Soviet Russia, women's physical strength will be adequate for the work allotted to them. This is not an 'argument' but a statement of observable fact – one of those coins of significant truth that can be extracted from the rubble of traditional attitudes and prejudices.

Yet according to the anthropologist Margaret Mead, however male and female functions differ from culture to culture, men's jobs always have the greater prestige (and no doubt pay). Cultures that she has not investigated might disprove her generalization, but in all the cultures from which we in the western world today have drawn our pattern of society, Greece, Rome, Christendom, women were the Second Sex. Why? What gave men their dominance over women? What made the women choose, or accept, submission? Some young Liberationists nowadays seem to think that a fundamental aggressiveness in the male psyche made them *force* women into subjection and that the discovery of the father's role in procreation and the rise of property consciousness reinforced the urge to possess. There must also have been a *fear* of women, of their power to inflame desire, and of their mysterious monthly flow of blood, which made men use their strength to circumscribe women, to repress them, even to revenge themselves on them. One of the nastiest chapters in human history is the way a celibate Christian priesthood blamed the torment of their sexual abstinence on the loathsome, devilish, carnal nature of Eve the temptress. That this dark strand in the male subconscious has persisted to our day I think is unquestionable. It is a curious fact that though women are sometimes accused of being 'man-haters' there is really no equivalent in our language for the much commoner 'mysogyny'.

Perhaps this question which bothers me almost obsessively, as to how women came into subjection, matters less than I think it does. Though it is obvious that through recorded history women who have needed protection and maintenance for themselves and their children have clung to men, women, with or without children, who were set by circumstance in the seat of power have *used* power. Elizabeth Tudor and the Empress Catherine of Russia toyed with men – but used them rather than were used. The biological imperative does not seem to have been imperative when women did not need dependence and were able and willing to wield power.

But at this point I must back-track to the time where I came in. How has the mood of women changed since 1928 when they were able in this country to vote for the first time on the same

terms as men? And why? It is not quite true, as is often supposed today, that the feminist movement ran out of steam in
the thirties. Women teachers and civil servants went on nagging
about equal pay and the marriage bar, for example. It jolts
even me a little to recall that in 1931 I was writing in the *Bolton
Evening News*: 'Why if it is admirable for a woman to devote
her time to public (i.e. voluntary) service, is it wrong for her to
engage in paid work?' At that time, of course, many private
firms, as well as government departments and local authorities,
required a woman to resign on marriage. I myself thought it
wise to sound the view of the editor-in-chief of the Co-operative
Press before I married. I was in the public gallery of the Manchester City Council Chamber when a motion to permit women
to continue to teach after marriage was carried. It was a notable
victory, for at that time there was widespread unemployment
and great bitterness at the idea of two incomes going into one
home. In the thirties, too, the women's organizations were cam-
paigning vigorously for many of the reforms which became the
foundation of the Welfare State. I don't think it is too much to
say that women's participation in public life, even before they
got the vote, and still more so when they were enfranchised,
contributed very greatly to preparing the climate of opinion for,
and getting through Parliament, many of our wide-ranging
social welfare provisions – as well as improving the position of
women in relation to divorce, married women's property and
the guardianship of children.

I identified with the campaigners of the thirties and I identify
with the campaigners of the seventies. The women who often
seemed alien to me were those in the fifties who turned their
backs and closed their minds to The Cause. There were not, of
course, after World War II the mass sackings that happened
after World War I to whip the women to anger – the reverse, in
fact. Women's work was so much needed in schools, in the
expanding social services, in shops, offices and factories that
women were begged to return. But this conflicted with another
very strong pressure on women – to become mothers and home-
makers. The birth rate always rises after a war. It is as if there
were a race impulse to assert the Life principle over the Death
principle. There must be an impulse, too, to retreat to the
warmth, security and comfort of home life after the danger and
bleakness of the war years. What was so sadly bothersome to
old-type feminists like me then is now perfectly understandable.
The march of the graduate girls and other highly educated
women into domesticity was inevitable. They had, unlike most
of their mothers, the choice of career or family life and they
chose family life, either because they admired their mothers'

domestic pattern; because they were rebelling against career mothers; because living-in domestic help which had enabled their mothers at least to engage in extensive voluntary work had vanished; or because they thought it was their duty.

It was in 1952 that Dr John Bowlby's World Health Organisation monograph *Maternal Care and Mental Health* was published, and the name Bowlby became synonymous in the fifties and sixties with guilt feelings about the risk to children of deprivation of constant maternal care. It was, in any case, time for a swing in the pendulum of ideas about child care; a re-action against the rigid, undemonstrative regime advocated by Dr Truby King which was miserably and half-reluctantly followed by mothers right up to my time who would really have preferred to feed on demand and cuddle and kiss, and rock the cradle or pram. During the years since Truby King, a great deal had been learned about infant responses and child pyschology. So Dr Bowlby's study of emotional deprivation in infants in institutions was fastened on as a sort of proof that all babies needed the round-the-clock care of their natural mothers and that there was a sort of mystical tie between mother and child. I doubt if this was really what Dr Bowlby was saying, but it was what a good many women, and men, wanted to believe. There are still a good many people who believe that this in-tensive mothercare is the norm and that any mother who en-trusts the care of her young child to anyone else for even part of the day is doing something outrageously abnormal – though it would be hard to find a previous period in history when the hour-by-hour care of children by the mother was thought necessary, or even desirable, in families where living-in domestic help could be afforded, or was possible in poor families where quite young children, as well as both parents, had to work or go hungry.

But there it was. The post-war generation of mothers were convinced, or convinced themselves, that without this kind of mothercare their children would be likely to become emotional cripples or delinquents. (Hard luck on the Royal children, I used to say. How could I feel otherwise, having had a working mother and a working mother-in-law?) The mothers I am talking about were, of course, the well-educated ones, the women who read their Spock, their Bowlby, their Winnicott. The others, in increasing numbers, took gladly the opportunities of earning money and finding company in shops, factories and canteens and did so without the guilt that haunted middle-class women, and without fear of the risks to 'latch-key' children which were sternly and frequently voiced by child psychologists, social workers, magistrates and the rest. (If they had been subject to guilt feelings, they would have been absolved by the knowledge that their earnings enabled them to make their homes more comfortable, buy their children better clothes and treat them to a few 'luxuries' which most middle-class people took for granted.) But the others, 'the whining graduate housewives' who were thought to be typical *Guardian* readers in the early sixties, could not shake off their guilt. They had *chosen* to be good wives and mothers; they loved their husbands, their homes and their children. Then why should they not be perfectly happy and fulfilled? Why should they talk, trying not to sound self-pitying, of being 'cabbages'? Why should they feel all screwed up, tied day after day to housework, and to little children whose need to acquire verbal and physical skills made inexorable demands on their mental and physical energy? Were they, many must have wondered, *monsters*, because the beautiful role of calm and patient cherisher, comforter, educator, inspirer, seemed outside their powers?

I think English women of this period stood up remarkably well to the dual pressures on them – to concentrate on 'ideal' motherhood and to fill the gaps in the schools, the hospitals, the social services. Whatever the poor mother felt it her duty to do, she was shot at from the other side, the 'stay-at-home wives', in my *Guardian* experience, being the more bitter and hostile. But in America the pressures were even more acute, the results, apparently, much more troublesome. I quote from Alice Rossi in an article in *Daedalus* in 1964:

'If a woman reads an article by Dr Spock on working mothers, she is informed that any woman who finds full-time motherhood produces nervousness is showing "a residue of difficult relationships in her own childhood"; if irritability and nervousness are not assuaged by a brief trip or two, she is probably in an emotional state which can be "relieved through regular counselling in a family social agency, or, if severe, through psychiatric treatment"; and finally, "any mother of a pre-school child who is considering a job should discuss the issue with a social worker before making a decision".'

At this point Alice Rossi comments tartly, 'Since the social worker shares the same analytic framework that Dr Spock does, there is little doubt what the advice will be: the woman is left with the judgement that wanting more than motherhood is not natural but a reflection on her individual emotional disturbance.'

But at this point, in 1963, Betty Friedan had come in, with her *The Feminine Mystique*, and the new revolt of women, which we now call Women's Liberation, had been born. When I read this book I had no idea how seminal it was to be. Neither, I think, had Eleanor Timbres, the American wife of my friend John Rosselli, who reviewed it for the *Guardian*. Probably because *Guardian* women readers who were my yardstick were coping with their pressures without feeling a need to resort to the psychiatrist's couch I thought it was rather hysterical. Could it be true that American women were having baby after baby in the hope of proving to themselves that they were 'true women', and that when this left them still mixed up, resentful and miserable, they were running to the psychiatrist? Could it be true, as Betty Friedan asserted, that market researchers, finding women working outside the home were 'a hard sell', were advising manufacturers to endeavour through their advertising, and through pressure on the women's magazines, to manipulate the attitudes of women towards a more domestic and 'homebird' image? It did not seem to me that women could be so easily manipulated as that. But when I read the book again, in 1971, one passage leapt out at me – Mrs Friedan's account of the experience of a New York analyst, trained at Sigmund Freud's own Psychoanalytic Institute in Vienna.

'For twenty years,' he said, 'I have found myself in the position again and again of having to superimpose Freud's theory of femininity on the psychic life of my patients in a way I was not willing to do. I have come to the conclusion that penis envy simply does not exist. I have seen women who are completely expressive, sexually, vaginally, and yet who are not mature, integrated, fulfilled. I had a woman patient on the couch for nearly two years before I could face her real problem – that it was not enough for her to be a housewife and mother. One day she had a dream that she was teaching a class. I could not dismiss the powerful yearning of this housewife's dream as penis envy. It was the suppression of her own need for mature self-fulfilment. I told her, "I can't analyse this dream away. You must do something about it." '

The need for 'mature self-fulfilment'; Mary Wollstonecraft's 'character as a human being'. *There* is another coin of significant truth dug out of the mud of traditional attitudes. Maturity means the capacity for independent thought, the capacity to question, decide, take action. Why have we, since 1870, been educating girls if we did not believe they had minds to educate? Of course the pragmatic aim of all state systems of education is to fit children for their place in the existing society, to condition them to the roles society expects them to fulfil, but its more profound aim, recognized now, as it scarcely could be in the class-bound 1870s, as applying not only to an elite but to all human beings, is to train the mind to think, to reason, to

109

imagine, to leap forward from accepted premises to new concepts. If you educate girls to *think* you cannot circumscribe their thinking. They will inevitably work out for themselves what 'mature self-fulfilment' means for them and if it does not mean relating all their values, all their attitudes, all their behaviour, to male concepts, men should neither be surprised nor resentful. If men believe that we are happier, more fulfilled, by a special 'feminine' form of education based on our 'aptitude' for the arts, including the domestic arts, our interest in the personal rather than the abstract, they may be right or they may be wrong, but they should certainly question their right to impose their assessment upon us. Educating girls for a supportive role is, after all, mighty convenient for man, as Dr Edmund Leach, Provost of King's College, let out, probably humorously, in a speech at Keele University reported in July 1969. It was time, he said, that we stopped educating women like men and producing 'second-class males', because it was 'getting too difficult to get anyone willing to do domestic chores'.

I think, therefore I am. But what am I? Who am I? My husband's wife? My children's mother? Or Me, Myself? Some time in the sixties I had an anonymous poem from a reader:

> *Me, myself, is dead.*
> *I am wife to my husband*
> *I am mother to our sons*
> *I am daughter to my mother*
> *I am mistress to our dog.*
> *And there is nothing else of me,*
> *Nothing left of me.*
> *Me, myself, is dead.*

It was because *The Feminine Mystique* spoke to women like this that it made its extraordinary impact. If Betty Friedan had invented or grossly exaggerated the malaise of the American housewife, her book could not have become a best-seller. The soil was fertile, as it was for the later equally best-selling books of Kate Millett and Germaine Greer. The malaise they identified was more feverish in America, but it existed here too. In America, much more than here, girls were awaking to the fact that on the campus they were expected to be 'men's girls'. All reports suggest that when young women threw themselves idealistically into the campaigns for Civil Rights for Negroes they were expected to do the traditional female tasks. The sting was sharp. 'Mature fulfilment for black men', but what about 'mature self-fulfilment for women, whether black, white or khaki'? (Shirley Chisholm, candidate for the American presidency in 1972, put it on record that she felt more disadvantaged as a woman than as a black.)

That was how Women's Liberation was born. Not only the troubled wives but the startled girls, were forced to ask themselves the question, 'What am I? Who am I? Am I a man's girl? Or Me, Myself?' Something in the conventional pattern of attitudes of men to women, women to men, was causing them severe discomfort. They were forced to question whether the pattern was really 'natural' and immutable. The girls had read their history – they knew that upper- and middle-class Victorians had lived comfortably within a pattern, that the division between rich and poor was divinely ordained, that now seemed ludicrous as well as unjust. Might there not be something equally ludicrous and unjust about a pattern which assumed that men were leaders, women followers, the 'boss, Girl Friday' pattern? Women's Liberation was born under the sign of the Question Mark.

So of course when I first began to hear about the Women's Liberation movement on the other side of the Atlantic my ears pricked, my nostrils quivered. I had been questioning assumptions about the male role, the female role, all my adult life. Weren't there more questions that I who counted myself a liberated independent female (chiefly because of an exceptionally 'equal' partnership in marriage) ought to be asking? Was this a carry-through of the suffragettes' fight for the vote as recognition that women were adult citizens? After years of retreat from The Cause, were young women really beginning to surge forward towards the goal of 'a character as a human being', or was this no more than a backlash to American society's obsession with sex? I was conned, as we all were, by the mass media myth of 'bra burnings' – an image that still persists and is seized on by men and women alike as an excuse to write off Women's Liberation as hysteria – but even if women did really publicly burn their bras and drop their false eyelashes into trash cans, wouldn't even this have been an understandable dramatization of the revolt against American society's assumption that a girl's success was to be measured by her ability to attract men; that if she didn't take pains to be sexually alluring she must be maladjusted?

In an account of an English group's 'consciousness raising' session I read the best description I have come upon of what Women's Liberation is all about: 'The skin over our eyes is peeling back.' When the 'skin' (traditional assumptions) is peeled back, the eyes register a quite different image and the change of focus can be a revelation. Imagine, for instance, Woman making God in *her* own image. Imagine what psychiatric dogma would have been if Freud had been a twentieth-century black Christian *female*. The mind boggles and it should boggle. If the concept of the stars revolving around Earth had to be questioned, so should the concept of woman's life revolving around the life of the man.

Here are three illustrations of how 'blinkered' most of us still are:

In a Six Point Group pamphlet *In Her Own Right* the Rev. Elsie Chamberlain reported a conversation between a little boy and a little girl about who was to be the preacher at their church next Sunday. 'It's Mr So-and-So', said the little girl. 'Don't be silly,' said the little boy, accustomed to the idea that the minister at their church was a woman, 'you know that men can't be preachers.'

In the *New Statesman*, Mervyn Jones told a story going around in New York of a man being killed in a car crash and his son rushed into hospital. In the operating theatre the surgeon exclaimed, 'My God, it's my son.' It took even me a moment to realize that the surgeon was a woman, the boy her son.

At a dinner given in her honour by the Fawcett Society, repository of the women's suffrage movement, Barbara Castle, then Minister for Employment, told how when she was getting ready for an evening reception, she could say to her private secretary, 'Would you please zip me up the back?', and he would reply politely, 'Certainly, Minister.'

Do these anecdotes alert the reader's mind to the fact that we have been wearing blinkers? There are plenty more questions that happy wives and mothers and deeply satisfied 'career' women who have the support of loving husbands (and the loving emancipated husbands themselves) should be asking. People who have said 'It stands to reason that a woman can't do that', or 'It takes a man to do that' must surely have noticed that now women are doing 'that', whatever it is, without fuss or difficulty. In Manchester, as I write, 54 women are driving buses. Women are reading TV, B.B.C. and commercial radio news and presenting more and more TV programmes. Women have been admitted to the Stock Exchange, have ridden on the race course in competition with men, been ordained Methodist ministers, sat on the Woolsack. Women in Fakenham, Norfolk, proved they had the brains and energy to keep production of leather goods going when their firm decided to close their factory down.

Just a handful of pointers to show the way our society is moving . . . and this time, there will be no backward swing of the pendulum. We shall *have* to accept that if Golda Meir could be prime minister of Israel, and Indira Gandhi prime minister of India this is a responsibility that some equally brave and experienced woman could undertake in Britain, or in Germany, or in France, or even as president of the United States. And there is nothing in logic to prevent a woman from becoming Lord Chancellor, chairman of the Bank of England, editor of a national newspaper or director-general of the B.B.C. Nothing in logic . . . only in traditional attitudes (which, of course, affect women's image of their potential, as well as men's).

The advance of public opinion has not happened solely because of the success of a few women in a few fields. It has been pushed along by a few women as dedicated to the cause as the Pankhursts or Millicent Garrett Fawcett. Activists in the more traditional women's organizations, the Fawcett Society, heir of the women's suffrage movement, as well as women's liberation workshops have done a great job of 'consciousness raising'. Women in Media, a specialist group allied to the Women's Liberation movement, has often been a spearhead. There is no question that it has moved attitudes to what jobs women can fill at the B.B.C., and has modified the derisive, patronizing attitude of Fleet Street and the world of broadcasting.

Equally certainly it was the demonstrations Women in Media organized, with immensely effective publicity, along with the lobbying of the liberation workshops and traditional women's organizations, which secured a Second Reading of Willie Hamilton's Anti-Discrimination Bill in February, 1973 – just a year after the defeat of the 1972 attempt, of which I wrote at the beginning of this chapter. From that time on, all parties accepted the inevitable and a Bill sponsored by the Labour Government passed through both Houses. Opposition was limited to details and the women's movement, though by no means satisfied, accepted that at least the Act due to come into force at the end of 1975 was a useful start. People say 'you can't change basic attitudes by process of law.' True enough, but if, for example, it becomes illegal to advertise for a 'dolly bird secretary', the boss men who assume that they have a natural right to a sort of 'office wife' will obviously have to take a new look at the roles of men and women. Legislation is a necessary basis for educating employers, unions, political parties, schools, colleges and many other institutions as well as the general public to the lack of logic, as well as injustice, in their attitudes and practice.

It is rather difficult for me to understand how other women

113

fail to see the limitation of the rights and opportunities of women as I see it. But I ought to bear in mind how much I have learned in the last four years by working in the Women in Media group. No one who has not been involved in an all-women group of *peers* – that is to say, women with similar work experience and attitudes – is likely to be able to imagine what a revelation it can be of how one's attitudes were always conditioned primarily by men; how one related one's image of oneself and one's potential to men's; needed to win their approval, and questioned one's judgement if it conflicted with theirs. I could never now subscribe to the notion that women are more difficult or temperamental than men, nor accept that they have less aptitude for leadership, organization or drive. Still less could I accept the Lionel Tiger view (in *Men in Groups*) that women do not 'bond'. They bond with a gaiety as well as tenderness that men's bonding groups could certainly not surpass. I wish I could convey to the able, distinguished women who broadly support the 'women's rights' movement but stand aside from personal involvement in it, what a life-enhancing experience this can be.

There are unforgettable memories . . . a torchlight procession organized by Midge McKenzie for Women in Media from Parliament to Downing Street in February, 1973. I walked alongside Mikki Doyle, dedicated Communist, women's editor of the *Morning Star*, and Dr Una Kroll, medical practitioner and ordained deaconess of the Church of England. In all the newspapers next day there were photographs of women's faces lighted up by the flares . . . not angry harpies, nor shrill fanatics but beautiful, *happy* women, like Georgia Brown, Midge McKenzie, Shirley Conran. Or the moment when, trooping down from the public gallery in the House of Commons after Willie Hamilton's Bill had won its second reading, we hugged and kissed (like footballers!) in the Central Lobby. 'We've done it. Oh we've done it.'

One stows these experiences away in the memory bank to draw on when the steam seems temporarily to have run out; when respected colleagues sniff disapprovingly, 'How humourless and obsessive you lot are'; when men (still) say winningly 'Have you burnt your bra?' or 'You really think like a man'; when other Liberationists with a more Marxist or Radical Feminist outlook accuse us of being 'elitist' (whatever that may mean), separatist, or 'middle-class'. The remembered glow of our achievements has stopped me worrying even about this kind of hostility. Every wing of the women's movement must do what it has to do, and must not be diverted or weakened by hostility, any more than by derision. What Women in Media decided it had to do, in August, 1974, was to run a Women's Rights candidate in the next General Election. We judged the time ripe, and the gesture important, to impress on all parties that women were not prepared to wait upon the pleasure of any government to pass anti-discrimination and equal opportunity legislation. Their unanimous choice of candidate was Una Kroll, a woman of first-class intellect, great experience of public speaking and broadcasting, warm sympathies, great insight . . . and the happy wife of an ordained priest and mother of four children. Una campaigned bravely and steadfastly for the ordination of women, but the brick wall that seems in the Anglican Church to confront women who yearn to participate fully in the life of the Church and its sacraments turned her mind to the wider women's movement. 'She can't be faulted,' we said to one another. 'She is so respectable and respect-worthy.' 'No one,' giggled another, looking at her lovely matronly figure, 'will dare to ask if she has burned her bra!' In electoral terms Dr Una's campaign was a painful failure. In terms of nationwide publicity, sneer-free, serious, even respect-ful, it was a resounding success. It raised the consciousness of very many women.

Why so much fear of the Women's Liberation label? Why is it so much of a threat, to women as well as to men? One meets and hears scores of women who say 'Of course, I'm not Women's Liberation, but . . . ' And the 'but' invariably refers to some discrimination, indignity or deprivation about which Women's Liberation workshops campaign assiduously. It may be having to get one's husband to sign one's income tax return; being refused as a guarantor for a nephew's TV hire purchase agreement when an eighteen-year-old male student is accept-able; it may be the shocking administration of the 'cohabitation rule' which deprives widows of their pension book and deserted or unmarried mothers of their supplementary benefit on suspicion of going to bed with the lodger; or the shortage of child care places; or the quota system of medical schools which keeps out British girls, though we are so short of doctors that we have to recruit them from the Third World countries (which need them very badly themselves); or having to pay for the Pill or other forms of contraception. Or any one of hundreds of indications that this is still a man's world.

I am absolutely certain that there is no recorded incident of 'bra-burning' in this country. What's more, there have been very few angry demonstrations; there is precious little of what even the most 'trad' homebody wife could call man-hating or hysteria. There is, and it had better be discussed openly, a strong feeling in the Liberation movement that it is necessary at present

115

to exclude men from conferences and discussions. I support this, because my experience with Women in Media has convinced me that in this present transition phase we need to be on our own to appreciate the power that is generated by women learning to work together. I do not go along with the view of other Liberationists that 'female is best' (like 'black is beautiful'), and though I do not morally disapprove of the many women who are now exploring physical relationships with their own sex, finding them, they tell me, more tender and supportive than heterosexual relationships, I am not one of their kind. I want to see women grow more confident and able to walk side by side with men in equal partnership. I want men to learn to shed their dark, age-old fear of becoming subservient to women, just as I want women to shed their fear of being un-lovely to men. Most of us in the women's movement say with total conviction that what we want is 'people's liberation'.

So I think again of my granddaughters, who are my hope for the future, and I trust that I shall have done my small bit to secure that they will not be prevented on the ground of being female from doing whatever is in them to do. I hope they will not feel it necessary to devote a major part of their time and their income to beautifying themselves in order to be attractive to men. I hope they will enjoy 'treating' as much as being treated, extending chivalry as much as receiving it and will feel comradely to women and comradely to men. I hope they too will marry and have daughters . . . and perhaps they will breathe such free air that they will wonder what on earth their great grandmother was fussing about.

9. HOME SWEET HOME

I wonder that 31 Highfield Street, Leicester, the house in which I grew up, did not kill my poor, thin, un-domesticated mother. Perhaps it did, for four years after we moved to a slightly less monstrously demanding house she succumbed, in five days, to pneumonia, aged fifty-seven. We kids loved the house – it was in a Victorian terrace, and had dining-room, breakfast-room, large kitchen and scullery on the ground floor; music room (drawing-room to other people), large bedroom, writing-cum-sewing-room on the first floor (reached by a back staircase chiefly used for the storage of home-made herb and chilli beer which sometimes used gloriously to explode); three bedrooms on the second floor, and above all this, one small attic where first the succession of maids and then my brother John slept, and a vast playroom. All the windows were large; the elegantly plastered ceilings were too high to reach with any kind of cleaning device. The long passage, kitchen and scullery were tiled. The water was heated by a huge range with a back boiler which once burst and flooded the kitchen floor. John and I thought it was a great lark to paddle about in the warm water, scooping it into buckets. In the scullery there was a gas stove, a shallow stone sink and a copper for boiling the clothes. Not even a garden for comfort and joy – only a narrow backyard where there was a row of lime saplings and a triangle of stony earth where my brothers and I used occasionally to erect a tent and once grew some limp cabbages.

Oh, the house was fine for us. We played cricket in the yard; in the back entry was a swing where I occupied myself cheerfully trying to kick the roof if I was first home from school and could not get into the house. (I became a latch-key child at the age of sixteen, very proudly.) Next door there was a synagogue and my brothers climbed all over it. When our balls went over into the synagogue yard we used a clothes prop with a split end to trap them and haul them up. We had no trees to climb so we climbed along gutters. One day my mother came home to see Guy walking along the guttering at the top of the house with a four-storey drop into the street. Even I, not notably adventurous, would wriggle along the roof edge at the back of the house with a sheer two-storey drop into the next-door garden. Pity the children of the high-rise flats who have nowhere to climb; pity their mothers who dare not let them take all the physical risks that normal children must take. (My daughter has told me, since she grew up, some hair-raising tales of the tree-climbing I never knew about when she was young.)

In the cellar the boys fixed up a dark room. Remembering the frayed wires that connected the home-made lamp with a red glass front, it seems miraculous we did not electrocute ourselves, as we developed our plates and films. The prints were laid out in hypo trays in the bathroom. In the attic there was John's train set. In the writing-room there was mother's rag bag, from which I drew lovely scraps of material to cobble up clothes for my large family of dolls. It was a splendid place to grow up, and having so many rooms meant that we could always escape from one another and very seldom bickered.

117

But what a drain on the nervous and physical resources of a clever, gifted, sensitive woman, a natural musician, a natural writer, a natural leader; a very rare spirit with limited physical strength and no great aptitude for any of the housewifely skills even cooking. No doubt at all that my resentment that house work is still considered, by many men and women, to be a proper life work for every woman who chooses to marry and have children, derives from the remembrance of what my mother had to force herself to do.

Consider wash day: coal had to be carried up from the cellar to shovel under the copper. The copper had to be filled, bucket by bucket, from the taps over the sink. The bed linen, towels tablecloths, table napkins and all other 'boiling' articles had to be carried down, dumped in the copper, and when boiled humped out, heavy with water and put through a mangle with wooden rollers, rinsed in the sink, mangled again, pegged out in the backyard, brought in, folded (usually with the help of a child home from school for lunch) and later starched and ironed with a flat iron heated on the gas stove or the hob. As long as my mother lived all the washing was done at home. She said she liked it better than any household job, but goodness knows what it took out of her physically. There was so much more to wash than now – not only the bed linen and table napery but antimacassars, table runners, chair-arm protectors cushion covers: in our house all curtains and soft furnishings were exchanged at spring cleaning time for summer ones. Most of our underwear was woollen; there were no sanitary towels or tampons; wash day included coping with bloodstained, evil-smelling towelling diapers such as only babies use today.

In those days chamber pots had to be emptied daily into a slop bucket and carried down to the lavatory. Nothing was drip-dry, stainless or 'mini-care'. All the table silver had to be polished frequently or it turned revoltingly black; knives had to be cleaned and polished with red powder on a knife board (a job John and I shared rather acrimoniously after Sunday lunch). There were brass name plates and knobs on the front door (one of my jobs to clean, and we had two name plates, one for my father and one for my grandfather); dust-filled Venetian blinds had to be wiped; stairs and carpets had to be swept daily with dustpan and brush; the dusting and polishing of furniture never ended; the fireplaces had to be cleaned out daily, and black-leaded weekly. (Actually we had an unusual number of gas stoves, in preference to coal fires, but I wonder now that we did not expire of cold in the music room, which had a rather feeble gas fire at one end and a small, smelly oil stove at the other. John and I suffered very badly from chilblains, and his often broke and suppurated.) Lancashire housewives stoned their front doorsteps and mopped down the tiled path to the gate. At least my poor mother did not feel this was a duty convention imposed on her.

In my lifetime the amount of sheer hard physical labour needed to keep a house and its contents clean and decent has very greatly decreased. (What a revolting idea it was that elbow grease was the best polish, as if there was something virtuous in exhausting physical labour.) Even the amount of soot in the atmosphere has lessened – my most nauseating memories of house cleaning centre round the revolting sulphurous, sooty smell of curtains when at last they were taken down to wash, and the grey deposit on all the china not in daily use. Now almost every home has a vacuum cleaner, a washing machine, an electric iron. The majority have refrigerators instead of stone-shelved larders, constant hot water, gas or electric fires as a supplement or alternative to the dirt-making, work-making coal hearth. Yet I wonder how much less time the housewife of today spends in cleaning and tidying than the women of my mother's generation. They, after all, found time to knit, crochet and embroider, as well as for great baking, jam-making, bottling, pickling sessions. I think our mothers and grandmothers saved themselves quite a lot of the work we do by choosing paint and furnishings that 'would not show the dirt' and I am pretty certain that their houses were grimier than ours except for the few weeks after that mammoth spring clean when the heavy furniture was pulled out and all the dirt and fluff that had accumulated behind it was swept up and carpets were taken up and beaten by hand.

Here, I think, is one of the clues to why housework is such a ceaseless drag. If you *see* dust, smears, dirt, they shame and embarrass you; they fill you with guilt. A woman busy with children, a job, or any other activities will, quite literally, not see dust and grime, but our present passion for light paint, light-coloured floors and furnishings, makes marks and the build-up of dust and grime much more noticeable than they would have been to our mothers. But we *choose* our surroundings, if we can, unable, or unwilling, to assess what demands our box-for-living may make on us in terms of maintenance. As K and I chose our first marital home, Cliff House, The Cliff, Salford, because though somewhat decrepit, in a neighbourhood that had almost literally gone down because the Pendleton Fault had caused a small landslide in the bend of the river Irwell round Manchester racecourse, it was large and without doubt the most beautiful house I have lived in, with splendidly proportioned rooms, superb marble mantelshelves in the sitting-room and dining-room, great bay windows from which we could watch the November Handicap and other race meetings. We paid a rent of ten shillings a week and ten shillings a week rates and it never occurred to us as we spread our tatty bits of furniture around (mostly from my old family home) that to more house-wifely eyes it might seem shabby or ill cared for. The plumbing was always springing leaks, and I would hare down the road to summon aid from the husband of our elderly cleaner; or in the middle of the night I would hear an ominous drip from the cold water cistern and crawl out of bed to plunge my arm into the icy water to adjust the ball cock. The paint peeled off the outside of the house and K, having made up his mind to repaint it, fell off a ladder and gave up halfway. We were very blissful in our ignorance of what higher standards of home care would have exacted of us.

What our relay team of domestics did not do was not done, and was not noticed by us – only, perhaps, by the housewifely women of K's family. I was confirmed in my belief that the bigger the house the better. So was K, though he had grown up in much more confined quarters than I. It was he who, through-out our married life, was always dreaming of bigger and more beautiful homes, who pored through the house advertisements in *Country Life*. He carried round for years an illustrated cutting of a beautiful country house in Suffolk, and it was still in his wallet when he died. I dreamed of houses literally – of inspect-ing strange, exciting monstrosities, or of coming upon some unused, forgotten wing of the house in which I was living at the time. The excitement of these dream houses was in their possibilities, how I would make them look, what we could do there. It is significant, I think, that almost the last improvements we made to our Edwardian house in Heaton Moor, Stockport, were the modernization of the kitchen and bathroom, and that the first was the removal of the Art Nouveau coloured glass panels in the hall, sitting-room, study and bedroom windows. For the house was not primarily my workshop, as my main work lay elsewhere, but an ambience.

Our ambience. We always chose the new wallpapers, the new carpets, curtains, furniture together, by the process of eliminat-ing everything either of us did not much like until we both said, 'That's it.' It is hard to write of our shared pleasure in the creation of a home background – of our trendy adventures with modern wallpapers, glass, stainless steel cutlery, our occasional find in a junk shop – without sounding like an advertisement for gracious living. But the pleasure was real and important; it did add a grace to our life; it *was* an act of creation – the creation of emotional security and ease, as well as of

120

consciously savoured immediate satisfaction. I have had many other ways of expressing my creative impulses, but making a home has by no means been the least important. For many women and some men it may be the *only* possibility of artistic expression.

Now I am alone I still feel a need for an ambience to express and support my personality – colours, shapes, proportions . . . and the Things that are either beautiful or part of my history, and so a reassurance that I am still Me. I know that if I had to discard all these I should be diminished. And how could I bear a life without a permanent core? Or a life without a private place to take off the public mask? But living alone gives a sharp insight into what one gets out of a private place for living in relation to the time and effort needed to maintain it. While I have been writing this book I have put off, time and time again, the need to get things repaired; have seen the need to clean, polish and dust the Things and to deal with the clutter of cuttings, papers, pamphlets, as a temptation to let myself off the hook, rather than as a duty.

When, in 1970, I explored in the *Guardian* the demands of housework, a professional woman wrote:

'My own perpetual temptation is to go on doing some housework when in my real moral opinion I ought to be doing some writing, precisely because housework demands nothing of my higher abilities. Tradition sees to it that I am tempted to feel virtuous when I have cleaned the floor, and wicked if I am at my desk with the floor dirty. However, I know that though dirt is not nice, my writing, even if not that of a genius, is far more use to the world than having a clean floor. I think of this business of housework as a temptation, as an excuse for not buckling down to more demanding work.'

My sentiments exactly. Even for a single woman making a cost/benefit analysis of the work of maintaining a place to live is difficult to do honestly, because of the pressure of our traditional conditioning. But how on earth can you make a cost/benefit analysis of a *family* home? There is no way of balancing this frightful complexity of accounts. If you start by listing all your work-making things and rebelling against their tyranny, you come to the realization that some of them are friends rather than tyrants. But that's only a very small start. What about those monstrous workmakers, the family dog and cat, shedding hairs, scratching furniture, making paw marks and worse on your floors? Now I am alone I very much miss the company of a dog, but have to admit that life is very much simpler without. And then, coming to the crunch, what about the *people* in the

121

house, especially the children? They are the supreme work makers, with their motorways for miniature cars, their jigsaws, paper dolls, their mysterious collections, their white mice, tricycles, dolls' prams, cooking sets, building bricks, remorselessly flooding their surroundings wherever they are. It wouldn't be too difficult to balance the work–use account in a home if it were just for eating (some) meals, sitting and sleeping. Only then it wouldn't be a home.

Perhaps we could do without homes? We could sleep in dormitories if we didn't want a private place to make love; eat in communal restaurants if we didn't want a private place to share food with our own family and chosen friends; we could arrange for our children to learn through play in nurseries and activity centres; we adults could watch TV, listen to, or make music or practise other hobbies in activity centres, just as we go to clubs, parks, public baths, for tennis, golf, cricket, football, swimming. Perhaps one day we shall – but the prospect is so bleak that we are driven back to Square One. What is a place of one's own worth in terms of the work it requires? ('One' own' is a very important factor. It will be a very long time before 'ownership' is not felt as part of human dignity and worth.)

There is another factor in the accounts that young wives rebelling against being on a conveyor belt of cleaning, tidying, cooking, push out of their reckoning. Quite a lot of the work a home demands is really rather enjoyable compared with a lot of the things we do in shops, factories, offices. Washing up? Is it awful to confess that with a double sink and draining boards, endless really hot water and a stacking device I rather liked washing up and only bought a dishwasher because I feared K was spending too much time at the kitchen sink? And actually I think he quite liked washing up, too, as he liked preparing vegetables, because it was mind-resting and showed gratifying results for labour. (He always used a pocket handkerchief to polish the glasses. Waste of time that could be better spent or a small recharging of the batteries?)

Of course, most of us spend far too much time in polishing floors, furniture, silver. Too much polishing just builds up dirt but there can't be many women who haven't felt a quirk of pleasure at giving the house a treat, seeing everything gleaming and sweet-smelling. (It doesn't last long, but it lasts much longer than it used to, before the introduction of long-life polishes.) It strikes me as sad that my mother couldn't set the table for tea without spreading doyleys on every bread and butter and cake plate, for they all had to be laundered, as well as the damask table napkins and relay of tablecloths. She *made* the doyleys, too, and quite probably enjoyed using her fingers in this way, as other women enjoy embroidering table-runners, chair backs, cushion covers, pillow cases. I've never been a needlewoman myself, and am perhaps more glad to have escaped from the endless mending of socks and underwear, of frayed collars and cuffs, the turning of sheets sides to middle, the patching up of pockets, than any other household task. But even I have made curtains and cushion covers – not because it was cheaper, but because it was quite pleasurable.

As for cooking – once you are above the poverty level you need to do very little cooking unless you wish. Children dote on instant puddings and baked beans out of a tin, and sausages left to cook themselves in a frying pan, and fruit is much better for their teeth and their general health than puddings. (My mother's constant wail was, 'What can I give them for pudding today?') There is an immense variety of convenience foods, frozen, freeze-dried, tinned. The busy mother can put something nutritious, satisfying, appetizing on the table in minutes. But I remember . . . when my father-in-law died there wasn't any reason any more, because K had a weight problem, to make those gorgeous treacle sponges and jam roly-polys that he adored and I loved making. When our daughter ceased to be a schoolgirl there was no reason any more to make jams and jellies, and I loved making jams and jellies. Bought Christmas puddings and mincemeat are now of very high quality, but the ritual of stirring the pudding, the co-operative effort of chopping the candied peel, cleaning the currants, stoning the raisins, blanching and peeling the almonds, is one of my happiest memories of childhood. The smell of baking cakes and bread, of grilling kippers or bacon, is as fragrant as the smell of roses or freesias. No woman has to do these things now if she doesn't wish to, but they were work that gave pleasure, as does a great deal of what we call 'work'. In saving the time and effort they take, with what comparable satisfactions do we replace them?

The offering of food is probably the most acceptable way of offering affection and regard. The most heartwarming moment of the day may be when the children rush in from school shouting, 'What's for tea, Mum?', you tell them, and they chorus, 'Oh goody.' If you have guests you can send out for ready-prepared meals from the Chinese restaurant and they may enjoy the food just as much as anything you could prepare. But will *you*? The creation (I doubt if it is too big a word) of the meal is an essential part of the act of hospitality. The greedy friends who eagerly accept second helpings and mop around their plates with their bread are paying homage to your culinary skill and you love them; the 'pickers' are rejecting not only your food but your concern for their enjoyment, and you are affronted. (Concern and distress over the children who 'won't eat' is much less due to the fear they will starve, for it is almost always adolescents who starve themselves to danger point, than to the fact that they appear to be rejecting love.)

So there we are in Home Sweet Home with all our accounts unbalanced. Treadmill, or the luxury of free choice? Slavery for the wife and unjustifiable indulgence of the husband and children? Or, as begins to seem possible, a co-operative private enterprise? Of course we have a long way to go in reducing unnecessary labour – a suction device to cope with the dust and grime that filters in from outside is probably our most urgent need. We have to shake off guilt that our standards fall below those of our mothers – or neighbours. We have to learn to resist trendy work-making fashions like fitted carpets in bathrooms and even kitchens, wished on us by the women's magazines and their advertisers. In my lifetime we have come a very long way towards minimum household labour and I hope that by the turn of the century we shall have gone very much further still. But what we most need is the attitude the Swedes are trying to foster: 'Don't *lend a hand* to Mother. Home maintenance is just as much your job as hers.'

10. SOME LITTLE JOY

Once I wrote plaintively in the *Guardian* that nowadays it seemed impossible to write about happiness, without sounding either trite or wet. We don't have 'essayists' in our newspapers and periodicals now; we have columnists and they may be angry, sardonic, outrageous, cynical, even boisterously *funny*, if they can pull it off. But they must not prattle on about their own little pleasures for if they did, in these guilt-and-fear-ridden days, they would soon be writing for themselves alone. And yet happiness keeps us sane. And yet the human being's capacity for joy is what most sharply differentiates him from the other animals – you can explain even love in terms of our physical needs, but you cannot explain joy.

When I was a schoolgirl a joggety-jog verse of Masefield's got into my head and it will not go away.

Best trust the happy moments. What they gave
Makes man less certain of the fearful grave
And gives his work compassion and new eyes.
The days that make us happy make us wise.

I am sure there is a sense in which Masefield was right – grief makes us aware of our mortality. Joy, inexplicable, unsought, unseekable, gives us a fleeting glimpse of immortality and dissolves our miserably separate identity into the All. I think, therefore I am. I suffer, therefore I belong. I experience joy, therefore I am released from Me.

It is the most trite of truisms to say that you cannot ever succeed by trying to snare the bluebird of happiness. There is no metaphorical mescalin or LSD that will ensure revelations of delight. It may come as you are walking home from work and the sky is that thrilling 'electric' blue and the starlings are chattering as they settle on their high window-sill perches; or in the intense light just before dusk the white flowers are quintessentially white and leaves are quintessentially green. It may come as you do the evening washing-up and there is a blackbird singing. It may be George Borrow's 'wind on the heath, brother', or Wordsworth's golden daffodils or Brooke's benison of hot water, or Shakespeare's white sheets bleaching on the hedge, or Chaucer's 'small fowls that maken melodye'. Or the smell of a baby fresh from the bath; or the smell of baking bread, new potatoes boiling with mint, even a sleepy dog's coat. It may come on mountain tops, on beaches, in the fellowship of pubs or conference halls; even in the din of newspaper offices. Sometimes it may just be that one's metabolism is functioning perfectly, for one can be happy against all sense or reason.

No, you cannot command joy, any more than you can explain it, but through the things you do you can, so to speak, put yourself in a state of grace for receiving it. This chapter is about the things I have done – apart from my relations with human beings – which have put me in the way of experiencing joy.

The first was singing, which goes back as long as I can remember. I became conscious that singing was joy at the age of about six, in a primary school where the headmaster conducted morning prayers in the big central hall but the children stayed in their classrooms, one child holding open each classroom door. I held the door one morning and sang the hymn happily, but as unselfconsciously as a bird. 'You sing very nicely,' said my teacher. That destroyed the innocence of my singing but gave meaning to it. From then on I never stopped singing until at the age of about sixty my voice became a wheeze and a croak. There must, I suppose, be other activities as joyful as singing,

125

but I have no experience of them. When you sing, the body is the instrument, the mind directs it and the spirit gives it meaning. The whole persona is fulfilled. The music is you; you are the music. It puzzles me that instrumentalists tend to think of singers as inferior musicians. Perhaps because they cannot see the mastery the singers have over their instrument? You can't see where the note is that the singer produces. Not even the singer can tell you where it is. A tone-deaf girl once said to me, 'How do you know when you open your mouth what note is going to come out?' How do I? Who can explain? This production of the right note seems to me a more astonishing thing than being able to put the finger on the precise spot on the right string and draw a bow across it. Singing can, and indeed largely must, be learned by mimicry and quite stupid people can learn to sing – but that doesn't, for me, lessen the marvel that by the disciplined control of larynx, mouth, palate, throat, lungs, diaphragm, a singer can accurately place a whole cascade of notes and leap unerringly across great intervals. All done by the mind directing not wood, cat gut, metal, but one's own flesh and muscles!

Singing, I believe, is the oldest of the creative forms of self-expression. Tiny children 'sing' when they are happy, even if no one has sung nursery rhymes to them. Primitive peoples have mourning chants, work chants, religious chants; natural sounds ordered into a pattern. Almost everyone has this natural instrument for making music. (The people who say they haven't are mostly too inhibited, for one reason or another, to try to use it.) You sing because you are happy, you are happy because you sing. But if you have the luck to recognize that this pleasurable sound-producing mechanism is an *instrument* the excitement begins of learning how to use it. The natural voice can do a lot, but how much more can the trained voice do. Untrained you can belt out 'Swannee River' at a party, carol 'I could have danced all night' in your bath, wallow in the full-throated sound of 'Land of Hope and Glory' at a Prom finale. Ah, but once you have learned to discipline your whole breathing apparatus so that your voice will move evenly up and down your natural register (and that is far beyond what in your untrained days you thought were your limits) you can transmit through your own body a large slice of the vocal music of the whole western world. There's riches for you. There's an invitation to the purest joy.

I learned the 'feel' of Brahms, Mahler, Sibelius, Strauss, Schumann, Mozart, Handel, Purcell, Bach, Schubert, Fauré, Wolf and even Britten, not through assiduous concert going and listening to records, but by singing their songs and arias. I have too, what amateur instrumentalists often miss, the 'feel' of the Magyars, the Finns, the Serbs, the Irish, the Scots, the French, the Germans, the Italians – and, my goodness, the Negroes – through singing their folk music. You don't need to have Civil Rights explained for you if you have sung 'Go Down Moses', or Is Massa Going to Sell us Tomorrow?'. Playing the viola or the oboe doesn't give you that kind of insight. Nor is playing the cello or the clarinet as likely as singing to bring you to an under- standing of unfamiliar new music. I came to Benjamin Britten by way of listening to Peter Pears singing his 'Michelangelo Sonnets' on records, buying the printed copy and sitting at the piano with it. The tessitura was too high for me, the piano accompaniment too difficult, but I *understood*, and have been able to go along with Britten in all his later development. It would be interesting to know how many 'cellists of a similar very moderate standard of accomplishment to mine would go out and buy Britten's 'cello sonata (and find an equally enterprising amateur pianist) and would work away at it at home, for their own pleasure, with no thought of impressing an audience, which was how my own singing mostly was – solitary, blissful, ecstatic, with Purcell's 'Dido's Lament', acres of Schubert and Schumann, acres of Bach and Brahms; the Ernste Lieder, the Dichterliebe, the Winterreise, the Wolf 'Mignon' songs. I know it is pure self-indulgence to go on. . . .

My native, inborn musical equipment is nothing remarkable. I had three advantages, being born into a music-loving family, having a voice of pleasant quality, and meeting with Elisabeth von Hedervary, with whom I sang gratefully for nearly thirty years. I went to her first in 1941 when K was called up into the Navy, thinking a few singing lessons would take my mind off the loneliness and anxiety. I continued to go to her once a week until I moved from Manchester to London in 1970, and in her studio I had some of the most perfectly happy hours of my life. Elisabeth is a wonderful teacher, and still teaching at the age of over ninety as I write. She came of an aristocratic Hungarian family and herself had the title of baroness. Rather against her family's wishes she became a concert singer in Vienna, who sang for Mahler, was a friend of Bartók and adored by Bartók's friend Bela Reinitz who wrote hundreds of songs for her. She fled to England when Hitler invaded Austria and has been teaching here ever since. She not only gave me command over my voice but vastly widened my knowledge of song. Our under- standing was so close that many times when I arrived for my lesson with Schubert, Dvořák, or Wolf under my arm she would say, 'I was thinking this morning I should like to hear Wolf (or whatever) again.' I was singing away joyfully when

I first felt my baby move. There was a day when I sang Bach's aria 'Seufzer, Tranen' with an English violinist and a Hungarian pianist and we all hugged and kissed, starry-eyed, in gratitude for the lovely sound.

So is the joy of singing narcissism, then? It could be, if one sang only solo, though the really great singers, like Kathleen Ferrier, Victoria de los Angeles, Elisabeth Schwarzkopf, Janet Baker, are always obviously intently listening and sharing. But the amateur with any sense sings also in choirs for this broadens and deepens his musical experience. So I am thankful to have sung Bach arias, but still more thankful to have sung in the Bach St Matthew Passion, the St John Passion, and best of all, in the Bach B Minor Mass, one of the greatest works of man. Imagine the glory of it, from that opening tremendous, searing 'Kyrie' bursting on the hushed audience, to the miracle of the Sanctus, where the octave bass is like a great ladder leading up to some celestial region where the triplets of the other voices rise and fall like the pinions of angels. I use this extravagant imagery deliberately because plain words cannot convey the sense of awe that singing in this master-work has always given me. Awe and one-ness – that losing of one's own small identity in something incomprehensibly vast and beautiful which is the essence of Joy.

I have sung in almost every kind of choral group – a local ladies' choir where we had to suppress our giggles in an arrangement of 'Excelsior'; in a madrigal group whose members were all young enough to be my sons and daughters and met week after week in a schoolroom, not to prepare for a concert, but just to sing Dowland, Weelkes, Gibbons, Wilbye, Byrd, Morley; in the Hallé Chorus under Sir Henry Wood, Beecham, Sargent; with a group of friends in one another's houses to work through *Così Fan Tutte*; and under various conductors at the Dartington Summer School of Music. And what I have learned from this is that once in a while, not inevitably and by no means necessarily as a result either of assiduous rehearsal or of the brilliance of the conductor, the music inexplicably takes wings and soars into the ecstatic. It must happen with orchestras too.

This happened, for instance, at the end of my first visit to Dartington. The programme announced that 'a small auditioned choir' would perform Benjamin Britten's *A Boy Was Born*. K was giving me this week as a birthday present, and I wrestled with the problem of whether to risk not getting into the auditioned choir the first week, or playing safe by choosing the second week when the scheduled work, for all the choir singers was the Mozart Requiem. I chose the first week, little realizin how rash I was. On the Sunday of the audition the applicant gathered in the hot sun in the green and peaceful courtyard, awaiting their summons up a flight of wooden stairs to the barn-like studio where George Malcolm was auditioning. I had had a lot of experience in choir singing; I had gone over the score many times with a gramophone record and I felt fairly confident. I was, indeed, one of the couple of dozen selected but I had never sung with a purist like George Malcolm before and had no idea what a beating I was in for. At one point he asked each of us to sing a few bars solo. 'You had better not sing it,' he said coldly to me. 'You have a vibrato.' Most of the others were similarly put down. 'I don't know *what* Mr Britten will say,' he raged grimly. I retired to my room near to tears of rage and frustration until the comic thought struck me that this was, after all, the lovely holiday treat dear K had given me.

And what Mr Britten said, when he arrived next morning to take the rest of the rehearsals, was, 'It's rather a pretty thing, isn't it?' (He was nineteen when he wrote it.) He smiled; we smiled; the sun shone. We foreswore the bathing pools, the tennis courts, the tiltyard and the intoxicating herb border. We worked on that devilishly difficult last variation hour after hour in the practice rooms. So came the performance in the dark of Totnes parish church on our last night. I expect Mr Malcolm thought that final variation was awful. But when we sang 'In the bleak midwinter', there were people in the church who wept, and as those closing semitones vibrated together I knew I had played my minuscule part in realizing a work of genius.

For what I have received I am truly thankful – to Mr Britten, to Mr Malcolm, to Elisabeth von Hedervary, to all my singing friends and conductors – and to my parents and forebears and for whatever in my genes and chromosomes enabled me to sing.

It's a big jump from my grand passion for singing to my tiny flirtation with painting, and yet that has also been a fount of joy. I wouldn't have missed it for anything but I very nearly did. Just as I always knew I could sing, so I always knew I couldn't draw. My father's brother, Sidney Peirce Waddington, who was professor of harmony and counterpoint at the Royal College of Music, could never have frightened me off singing, but my mother's brothers, Harry and Leo, completely scared me off painting. They could; I couldn't. Leo earned a very good living as a book illustrator, deviser of book jackets and portraitist in chalk, crayon and pencil. I hero-worshipped him from the time he drew my doll 'Billy' in my autograph album. Harry was a good water-colourist and had a woodcut or two in the Royal Academy. But I, literally, couldn't draw pussy. The horror of having to draw an umbrella from memory in our Oxford School Certificate exam lives with me still.

My visual memory is almost non-existent. I very seldom dream 'visually', and never in colour. If asked to describe what Miss So-and-So was wearing at a party I am likely to say, 'Green, I think. No, it may have been blue.' That there are people who can turn on a mental switch and recall in precise detail of colour and shape what they have seen weeks ago is as mysterious to me as the idea of singing was to the tone-deaf girl. Mary Stewart, the best-selling thriller-writer told me, 'Sometimes I am only in the place which starts a book for a few days. But all I have to do is "to run the film through again".' K, like many technical journalists, could recall very precisely anything he had seen in print. Once we set off to visit some friends and suddenly realized that neither of us could remember the address. K switched on his mental camera, recalled a letter and 'saw' the address at the top of it. So it should have been he who took to painting – but it wasn't.

However did *I* come to do it? Before one of our holidays K, who had been ill, was advised by a friend to take a child's paintbox and dabble with it, as therapy. So we were in Suffolk, on the edge of Tunstall Forest, with the paintbox and I thought I would have a go too. There was a lane, and four fir trees and a red signpost and these I 'drew' in paint (no pencil, for remember, I knew I couldn't draw). And there actually was a picture. A View. I was over fifty and I had never, but never attempted a View before. It was a tiny revelation. Sadly, K, who painted several poster-like scenes which I thought charming, gave up. It was I who went on to enjoy my painting more and more, and would now never go on holiday without a paintbox.

This joy I share with hundreds, thousands, of English men and women of all ages and every class. It is a very cheering aspect of modern living to set against the tyranny of the gogglebox and the motor car. For years I pitied Victorian misses for being subjected to drawing lessons to add to their stock of pitiful little accomplishments. I thought it was very comical that my mother laboured away over her copy of a picture of chrysanthemums (though actually it made rather a pleasing fire screen). It was the sort of thing most of her Edwardian contemporaries were doing, mostly very badly. But now cabinet ministers paint; scientists paint; retired teachers paint; lots and lots of housewives paint. One of our daily helps, who worked for us for years, started going to an art class when she retired. She was an immediate success, soon had her pictures accepted for exhibitions, sold quite a few, and began to make friends and acquaintances in an entirely different social circle. There is something as natural, I think, in the impulse to make pictures as in the impulse to sing – and it is a good deal more respectable for a businessman to say he takes his paints on holiday with him than that he settles down to madrigals with his friends and family after dinner. Perhaps that will come, when a statesman as famous as Sir Winston Churchill has admitted to a passion for part-singing.

Among this legion of amateurs there must be some who have genuine talent which once would have been wasted. (No geniuses, however. They make their own way, without social encouragement.) The majority take to oils which is better as therapy, I imagine – sploshing all that lovely oozy paint about must work off a lot of neuroses. But, to K's disappointment, it didn't work for me – too timid with the big brushes, too mean with the paint. My oils were as thin as water-colours. I changed to gouache, for that, drying quickly and possible to paint over and build on, was much easier than water-colour which must be caught, so to speak, on the run. Now I have a little more skill and a good deal more confidence, I am attempting what I always really wanted to do – delicate, precise but evocative water-colours. A perceptive woman I met on a painting holiday said, 'Mary paints as if she were writing.' But of course. I am a 'verbal' person. If I could paint as I would, I should paint like the Chinese.

It must seem very perverse and wilful of me to be so resistant to the idea of being *taught* to paint. I do think that if I had started earlier and been made to 'practise' my visual memory might have been greatly improved. Lacking perfect pitch, I developed a very serviceable relative pitch. So my eye could have developed a compensatory skill, perhaps. I never learned to type properly, yet I can now proceed without looking at the keys. Though my piano playing is indifferent, I keep my eye on the score, not on my fingers. But however intently I look at a row of trees or buildings my mind's eye has forgotten it by the time my head bends to the paper. To fill a notebook with pencil sketches to translate into water-colours or gouaches at home would be impossible for me. So I ask myself, what am I doing in a painting class? They take it for granted – all artists do – that I have a basic equipment which I believe I lack, and that lack includes not only visual memory but visual imagination. What is any tutor to make of me, poor chap? In the present climate of opinion about the function of Art he is likely to say, 'Express yourself creatively' – which is just miserably frustrating and embarrassing if your mind doesn't tell your hand what to express. I could no more paint an 'abstract' than I could build a radio set. (Perhaps there are schoolchildren who would get a greater kick out of being helped to draw a convincing and fairly accurate picture of a car engine than out of sploshing colour about to 'express' themselves? I shouldn't wonder.)

So what am I doing sitting surrounded by my tubes of paint, my baby's plastic feeding bottle full of water, a rag, an old newspaper, a few tinfoil or plastic containers for mixing paint, a couple of sable brushes and a drawing pad no bigger than 14″ × 11″? Enjoying myself. Enjoying myself deeply and profoundly and storing up treasure. Just as I sang for myself, so I paint for myself, not to exhibit, much less to 'sell'. All that is left of the singing is a tape recording or two, but the little paintings, in simple frames so that they are easily interchangeable, are in clusters on my sitting-room walls. I think they look very pretty. I think they begin to compare with Uncle Harry's water-colours in the dining-room. But the most precious thing about them is that they are 'Me, there'. Phooey to the purist who say that I might as well have taken a colour snap of the red roses trained up a palm tree on the shores of Lake Maggiore as paint it painstakingly, representationally. It isn't true. You leaf through your colour snaps and wonder, 'Where was that?' but if you have sat for hours focusing your eyes on the scene you never forget. You bring every aspect of it home with you on a bit of paper or an oblong of canvas. From my supper I look up at the Parthenon and remember the chattering German schoolgirls who pestered me while I moistened my brush with spit because I had forgotten my water bottle. Or at the glory of the flowers mantling Delos and how, in a sudden panic, thinking of snakes, I gathered up my paints and ran. Or at an impossibly cobalt sky and wooden chalets in Trinidad, Northern California, where the tiny humming-birds whizzed in and out of the shrubs as the fierce sun scorched my neck. Or at the pearly pink sky and the black headland and rocks as I painted the midnight sunset, the cold paralysing my bottom, at Reykjavik, Iceland. Or the row of cypress trees against an austere hillside in Provence. The wind nearly blew me off the wall I was straddling, and the tutor asked, 'Why have you painted a graveyard?' 'Because it was there,' I said, but actually, I liked the little points of white the gravestones made. Or the peace of the Iken marshes on a sunny Easter Sunday, and the *Peter Grimes* sounds in the air on the seashore at Aldeburgh. Or my granddaughter Caroline daubing away beside me as I battled to get on paper the sun setting over the Channel from a bedroom window in Sussex.

Surveying my pictures with a knowledgeable but kindly eye, a friend said, 'They must be very nice souvenirs.' Absolutely right. But she didn't know the half. Could I put in a little plea

strong-minded enough to do this, you have to do the tidying up yourself, but you bitterly resent it. I never resented the march of the weeds.

So one of the superabundant joys of a garden is achievement: we made it, we grew it – with the aid of the sun and the rain and the soil and the birds and the bees and the worms and the Life Force. We planted (and pruned and weeded round) the raspberry canes, and the reward was walking down the garden and bringing up a dishful for breakfast. We planted the strawberries and layered them and put down slug bait, endlessly weeded round them and crawled in hot sun under the net, and brought up to the house a basketful that filled our largest soup tureen to overflowing. And there were the runner beans (*I never knew I liked them till we grew them*), the round white turnips, the purple sprouting broccoli, the new potatoes whose skin came off at the touch of a fingernail; the hundredweights of apples. Why does it always seem to have been an Indian summer when I scrambled up the apple trees and balanced in nervous excitement between the stepladder and the branches? And of course, the flowers – from crocus to daffodil to tulip; from stocks to nemesias to asters; from peonies to lupins to dahlias. And all the roses known by name as if they were children. The year went round very fast and everything died too soon but one could never forget the enduring quality of *life*, that there would be another spring – and another.

It is very hard to leave a garden. When you move house the essentials of home go with you, the furniture and books and pianos and china and silver; all the things that have strong emotional significance as well as use. But when you leave a garden all you can take with you is a few dahlia tubers, a few clumps of herbs, a small cherished plant or two, and so you leave something of yourself behind.

The daffodils and scillas, carefully replenished each year. The cherry, the nut tree, the two pear trees we planted. That straggle of white pinks breathing out the honey of summer. The Bourbons and Gallicas, pink and white striped, purple, crimson, violet; Mary Wallace, who climbing up the side of the house and almost peeping in the bedroom windows had about five days of glory every summer; Zephyrine Drouhin, Lavender Lassie, Elizabeth of Glamis, Wendy Cussons, Orange Sensation. In the Prince's Road garden a very comical and lovable dog, Ben Bassett, was buried. Sometimes I think a small part of me was buried there too, for since I wrenched myself away I have never experienced that flooding in of delight I sometimes knew there – perhaps just looking at the bridal white of the philadelphus, the triumphant blaze of those common self-seeded red

135

poppies, or the perfect formation of a dahlia or a rose. But perhaps some day, somewhere, in some other garden?

Singing, painting, gardening, these possibilities of joy are earned. Is the joy of holidays an uncovenanted benefit? Not quite, perhaps. On the face of it you need only a little money, enterprise and time, but some people seem to get such a little joy from their holidays, and I get, infallibly, such a lot that I think perhaps even with holidays you have to be in a state of grace to receive. I can remember some moment of unflawed pleasure from every holiday since at the age of ten I learned to swim in the bay of Hell's Mouth on the Lleyn Peninsula, and, climbing up the headland, saw the sun setting to the south and the moon rising to the north. So I travel not merely hopefully but confident that there will be something to add to the stockpile of treasure.

Other people may not be able to buy bliss. If what they want is a warm sea, hot sun, a luxurious hotel and gay company, their package deal may be no bargain. It may rain persistently, the beds may be uncomfortable, the food lousy, the company boring. Some people are so disenchanted that they even give up and run for home. But not me. There was a day on Rhodes when we went by coach to Lindos and it rained and rained and rained. The party huddled miserably in a café where the coach parked and I, restive, said to K, 'I think I'll just have a look at the village,' and walked on through the rain, round this corner and that, until I was in sight of the most beautiful Acropolis and raced up to the top, and raced even faster down in case I should keep the coach waiting. 'Where have you *been*?' they asked me crossly. 'To see the Acropolis. That's what we came for,' I replied.

Of course it is better, going to Greece, or any country with a long, long history, to have absorbed enough to know what to look for. To have read enough Greek history and myth, enough Homer, Euripides, Sophocles, Aeschylus – or, if you missed these in youth, enough Mary Renault, Leonard Cottrell – to know what you are seeing; to be able to stand on one bank of the great loop of the river of time and look across to the other side. The chasm between then and now can, for a flash, seem very narrow, if you are stroking the marble of the Parthenon or standing among the wild flowers of Delos or of Mycenae in the ruins of the chamber where Clytemnestra awaited the return of Agamemnon, or listening to the fall of a coin in the centre of the miraculous theatre of Epidaurus.

But the pleasures of recognition, of association of conscious self-exposure to the past, are not absolutely essential to euphoria. That comes as it will, inexplicably. You may expect to be awed by the Lion Gate at Mycenae and find that what moves you almost to tears is the custodian stepping quietly into the blackness of Agamemnon's tomb and gloriously chanting his prayers; or the piper piping across the valley. You may be soaked through with happiness in a Mykonos hotel dining-room surrounded by caged singing birds, plastic flowers and canned bouzouki music. Sun, wind and mountains are almost infallible for me, as when I was standing in the capitol gardens at Salt Lake City looking over the salt flats to the mountains and the Mormon Choir's hymns drenched the air, over the loudspeakers from the Temple in the town. But it happened in Stockholm, on a brilliant February morning when I walked on the frozen sea and saw that it *was* violet, just as the postcards show it. And when I was perched on a cliff in northern California amid a tangle of shrubs and flowers with the Pacific blotted out by a dense fog. Suddenly a mysterious black shape loomed, and another and another, quite frighteningly, and the mist lifted and the sun revealed huge craggy rocks on the shore. And in a strange, terrifying kind of way when I stood, on a beastly cold, drizzly night watching Hekla, the Iceland volcano, spewing out flame and lava from the bowels of the earth. Far from blissful yet a piece of genuine 22-carat gold to add to the treasure chest.

So there are the four great joys that this Mary had (they leave out the joy of human intercourse because that inevitably crops up all over the place in a book of this kind). And I have to ask myself, 'What makes the human animal capable of delight?' Whatever it is, it is not something that can be rationalized away by behaviourist philosophers in terms of 'good' smells, 'healthy' sun and wind, or the elaborate conditioning of the brain by poets, painters and historians to appreciate the picturesque, the well-proportioned, the antique. Admit this conditioning, as you must, for there are fashions in the appreciation of nature, just as there are in the appreciation of architecture, painting, dress and female beauty, and you still have not answered the question why the sight of a clump of primroses in a hedge makes us catch our breath. Because Wordsworth told us it was beautiful? Nonsense. A tiny child will stop, sniff and raise a radiant face to its mother, crooning, 'Pretty.' The mother may have shown the child this possibility of pleasure but she could not condition the response. The educated adult mind considers 'the simple primrose at the river's brim' and asks, '*Why* primroses, so useless, so unimportant? Why have they survived? Why do we delight in them?'

And why do we delight in the Parthenon, the Iliad, Chartres Cathedral, the Sistine Chapel, Hamlet, the Bach B Minor Mass, the Eroica symphony. And why has the naked ape, evolving into *homo sapiens*, always struggled to create artefacts that were not solely for his use, but for his joy?

11. AN END AND A BEGINNING

To write of how I learned to be a widow and eventually to stop thinking of myself as a widow is to risk the disapproval of some of the people whose opinion I value most. Yes, one should contain one's grief. But one of the things I have learned through all this is that we who have words can articulate grief for those who have not, and that to have grief spelt out, its pattern charted, is something we all obscurely need.

K died on 29th November, 1967. He was fifty-six. We were going through a severe family crisis which necessitated our compiling together a very difficult statement. K scribbled some notes and then said he felt unwell and had better go to bed. 'I'll finish it in the morning,' he said. 'Like hell you will,' I thought to myself, and sat down at the typewriter, running up- and downstairs every few minutes. 'I think you had better phone the doctor,' he said, about midnight. The doctor, a locum, said what pills to give him and to ring back if necessary. I showed K what I had written and he grinned. 'I only did this to get out of doing the job,' he said. It was the last thing he said to me. Good for me that his last words were a little joke. There came that dreadful rattle in the throat and though, of course, I phoned the doctor again I suppose I knew. I lay across him and put my mouth on his, but with a feeling of helpless inefficiency. What did I know about mouth-to-mouth resuscitation? The doctor came, very tall, very dark-skinned, very uncommunicative. A stranger. He gave me, I think, a sedative, and went away. It was three o'clock in the morning and I was alone in a very large house. I don't remember weeping. My one thought was that somehow I must get through the next three hours before I

138

could communicate with the outside world. There wasn't anyone I felt I could wake from sleep with this news, least of all my poor daughter. It never occurred to me that one could phone the undertaker in the dead of night. I know now that any woman could knock up her neighbour and get help, but all I could think of then was that about six o'clock I could phone K's nephew, Denys Stott, who made a very early start for work. I hope no other woman, stuck as I was, will think she has to wait to cry for help, even at 3 a.m. on a cold November morning. So I wandered up and downstairs, making tea and coffee, going in and out of the bedroom, to lay my head on K's shoulder or kiss his hands. There was nothing frightening to me about his still warm body. He was still my love. If I took a sedative – and I truly cannot remember – it induced not the smallest inclination to sleep. So I settled down to write letters to my friends. 'It was a strange letter,' one of them told me afterwards. I expect those letters *were* strange. I can remember writing in one, 'I feel a great life force in me.' Little I knew then that it was only a merciful illusion.

So at 6 o'clock I phoned Denys. 'Good God,' he said, and put the phone down. It is hard at first to realize that your friends are shocked too; that they too cannot speak for grief; that it takes a little time for them to be able to talk to you. Two hours still to go before I could venture to make the other phone calls, to our daughter, to K's friend and editor, to my friend the northern features editor, to Helen, my closest friend.

I scratched up the willpower to phone the undertaker and to dictate a telegram to my brother and that was my lot. I am glad I could cope rationally with what had to be done, but I think now that no woman should feel she has to drive herself to get out these dreadful words. Anyone, almost literally anyone, would do it for you, glad to be able to serve your need. The respect and tenderness for grief are universal, and the effect of shock is worse for many women than it was for me. I had the strong comfort of knowing that my husband had suffered scarcely at all (though who knows if there is a moment of intolerable agony in the moment of the coronary thrombosis?). I could say, 'Thank heaven you are out of it all, my poor love'; out of the pain of the family crisis, out of the misery of ill-health; out of the sense of the failure of his life's work at the death of the *News Chronicle.* I was not, I found, frightened of death itself. But many women are terrified, half out of their minds with fear and shock. They need someone to take charge and no one should hesitate to ask. They will not be refused.

So by nine o'clock help began to arrive. Denys, Alison Godlee, my very dear young neighbour, Helen, K's own good, kind doctor. I found I could cope with the undertaker because he was a plain blunt man from the Co-op who minced no words and did not sentimentalize over me. And I knew what documents he and the doctor needed and where they were to be found. It was then that a strange persistent obsession with the problems of all widows took hold of me. I pictured having to scrabble through K's drawers, even his pockets to find the papers we needed; I pictured having no money in hand to buy food, or even stamps. For God's sake, I wanted to yell, don't wait until it is too late to know where your husband keeps his essential papers; don't ever leave yourself short of a few quid in the Post Office or the bank. K died at the end of a month and there was £7 in his account – he spent as he went, I was the saver. I knew, too, what he would wish for his funeral. We had enjoyed many macabre jokes over funerals together. 'One pew nearer the front' he used to say, and once when he spoke the funeral oration for a friend, another journalist friend whispered to him as he walked back down the aisle, 'Can I book you for mine?' He outlived K. So I knew all about that, and that he would want his friends to be able to say goodbye to him in dignity and fellowship, and that though we were agnostics he would think it right that this goodbye should be in a church; that his good friend, Canon Wilfred Garlick, of St George's Church, Stockport, who was once 'Radio Parson' and a contributor to the *News Chronicle*, would help me. I even knew that K would want the sailors' hymn 'Eternal Father, strong to save' and that *my* goodbye must be the final chorus from the Bach St John Passion, 'Lie still'. The church was filled with men singing strongly and sturdily. It was as it should be.

On the day of K's death I wandered about clutching, for what reason is now beyond me, a shaggy white toy poodle belonging to my granddaughter, vaguely stroking it and holding it close. I think I drank a great quantity of brandy, which may have dulled my wits but certainly did not intoxicate me. My friends phoned, arranged, did instantly everything I asked, so that I had a curious feeling of behaving like a queen, for the first time in my life. I slipped away often to the bedroom to be alone with K for it seemed to me then that he was still there. But he wasn't. He was dead. His body would disintegrate. He was a job for the undertaker. I slammed the door tight on this thought for many weeks but there came a day when I walked down the garden and found a bird decaying and smelling evilly, caught in the cherry net. Then I knew what for me is the ultimate horror of death – not that our dear ones go elsewhere or that they cease completely to exist, but that the bodies they

140

have inhabited, the bodies they *were*, the bodies so precious to us, flesh of our flesh, are corruptible. *That* is why I cannot understand how any human being in his senses can deliberately reduce another human being to a carcase, a lump of inevitably decaying flesh.

So the funeral went over, which I remember very well, and the service at the crematorium, which I remember not at all, and my friends and family came from all over the country and wrapped me in kindness, and a brave handful even came with me to a little party K and I had planned, to hear and see Benjamin Britten's *Gloriana* at a local theatre on the evening of the funeral. It was harder for them than for me, for at this time one is still moving about like a zombie. The need, as they say in Lancashire, is 'to pass the time on', to get each day over, especially the rest of the day after the funeral. Two days later I went back to work. The thing to remember about bereavement is that one does what one must, and no one can imagine what this may be before it happens. I, who knew very well that the likelihood was that I would be a widow some day, had felt quite sure that if and when it happened I would run to my good friend Helen. In the event, I found that nothing would have dragged me away from the home which was, so to speak, the crown of our thirty years of happy life together. Other widows run away from their home in horror; a few never go back. But our dear house and garden, K's presence there, the friendship of my neighbours, proved the only strength I had. Unlike many bereaved women I was not afraid to go to bed alone at night – I had done that for most of the years of our marriage. And I did not really think out whether I *had* to go to work. That was the pattern of my life and it did not occur to me to wonder whether it should be changed. There were the letters to answer, two or three hundred of them. For a writing woman this may have been cathartic. For others it might have been an impossible burden, but I think that there are very few people who are not helped a little by having the 'condolence' letters. 'They are so hard to write', people say. 'Whatever can one say?' It doesn't matter much what, though it is best if one can say something in praise of the person who has died. The comfort lies in the fact that the pile of letters indicates your grief has some importance, however brief. You may need to go back to them again and again later when everyone else seems to have forgotten and you yourself are more afraid of forgetting than of remembering.

I think perhaps it is true, as people often say now, that we have pruned away too many of our mourning rituals; that we shuffle death out of sight too quickly and expect too much of the

141

bereaved in behaving rationally, discreetly, courageously. No blinds are drawn round the house of death now, as when my mother died. The funeral cars pass unnoticed – one of my keenest memories of my mother's funeral is the men on either side of the road raising their hats like puppets all the way to the crematorium. But I truly do not know where the answer lies. To make a parade of grief, to institutionalize its forms, as the Victorians did so grotesquely, is perhaps even worse than to treat death as a regrettable brief incident. I would sooner have gone to K's funeral in what I happened to have on than make a show of myself with crepe and veil and weepers. Suddenly I remember that I had my hair done, which was thought to be very brave and good. No doubt my appointment was due and I vaguely assumed I had better keep it. No doubt other women automatically make up their faces. To be noticeably lip-sticked or noticeably tear-blotched. Which is worse?

Grief is an illness of the psyche. To formalize opportunities for its release, for weeping, wailing, yelling at fate is unlikely to help. Tears don't come to order and if they did, how could they bring relief? Rage creeps up on you unawares too. I was coming back from London and as I walked along a crowded compartment and saw people laughing and talking and reading and sleeping something in my mind went briefly out of gear. Their normality was hideous to me. I was in hostile country, an enemy alien. Fortunately two friends were waiting for me at the end of my journey. The mental processes slipped back into gear. It does not happen so quickly for everyone. I used to say for myself that like Katherine Mansfield's poor 'Ma Parker' I had no private place to cry. It wasn't true, because I had a whole empty house to cry in – but so often the need for tears came when I was at work, when it could not be satisfied. The body's protest at this rigid self-discipline was the quite terrifying exhaustion that came over me at times, so that I could barely lift my hand from the arm of a chair. As with many another woman, the sense of loss sometimes manifested itself in a searing physical pain, somewhere in the guts. It might have gone more easily for me if I had not slammed the door as tightly as I could on recollection of what had happened – I came to think later that I had slammed it against K as well as against anguish – but at the time there was no question of choice. In grief we do as we must.

It seemed to me that I must not delay the sorting out of K's possessions, the giving away of his clothes. It is a brutal job of butchery of one's integrated life with another human being, and sometimes I moaned like an animal. Let no one think I blame any woman who cannot or will not face it for years. I understand very well the passionate clutching to oneself all that was 'his'. But I fortified myself with scorn for Queen Victoria who thought she could keep Albert with her by retaining round her all his things just as they were. The aura that personal possessions, especially clothes, take on from their owner, so dreadfully poignant at first, lasts a pitifully little while. I am sure I acted blindly, not rationally, but if I could have put it into words I should have said that I didn't want to become the maudlin custodian of a museum, for then, if the tears came, they would come only from self-pity.

Self-pity was easy to identify as the supreme enemy – easier for me, I dare say, than for many, because as a woman's page editor, I knew more than most about the problems of widows. 'Why did it have to happen like this to me?' could not be allowed, for I knew very well that there were three million widows in this country alone, and that for many of them it must have been very much worse than for me. No doubt my obsession with their plight, their lack of money, lack of job, of experience in standing on their own feet was part of my defence mechanism. I felt driven to write about 'Learning to be a widow' in the *Guardian* and to speak of it on BBC Woman's Hour. It was thought a very courageous thing to do, but the only thing that took a little willpower was controlling my voice as I read the scripts – and how tenderly supportive was my Woman's Hour producer. Putting things into words was my habit of life, the need to identify with the Three Million, to try to help the still secure to prepare themselves just a little for the state of widowhood, was a compulsion. In grief we do as we must.

My own basic problem was not money or security or health, it was simply learning, after thirty years, to live alone. The practical things were a bit troublesome, but few were impossible. What was so hard was breaking the habit of having someone to talk to – about the day's papers, what went on at work, the meals, the garden, the state of the nation, anything that came to mind. Even during all those years when K worked by night and I by day we had talked on the telephone very frequently and unfailingly at 11 o'clock at night. Even now I find it difficult to imagine myself into the life of the happily solitary people who feel no need to talk about what they have read, seen, heard, thought, to any other person. It wasn't, with me, that there was really no one to talk to – there were colleagues, friends, neighbours, and in the early days I understood very well the need to make it easy for them to talk to *me*, to protect them against the embarrassment that they might be 'intruding on my grief' or that I might burst into tears. (Though people really should not mind risking that. It's a very small thing to bear, having a weeping woman on your hands, compared with the release it may give her.)

It was a little later that it came to me that there was no one I could talk to as of right. When you are suddenly bereft of your 'speech-friend' (as William Morris called it) you fear that by engaging in conversation with anyone else you are asking a favour. Social assurance is more precarious than we think, for it rests on the assumption that by and large it is mutually agreeable. Gauche adolescents find it impossible to believe that anyone would actually enjoy talking to them; so do people whose inner security has collapsed, through bereavement, divorce, desertion, disgrace, being made redundant or any other reason. I began to have some insight into loneliness, the creeping paralysis of the social responses. All those letters from widows spelling out for me their sense of isolation, of being excluded from society, made me well aware of what the poor beggars were clutching at, and that I too might clutch too hard, might expect too much of my friends, might strain their kindness. I knew how the lone widow woman can erode the patience of a well-intentioned neighbour who has said kindly, 'Drop in any time,' and can become an old man of the sea. My own best help came from a friend who turned up almost every Saturday evening to play two piano duets, bringing the pudding for our supper in the boot of his car. I worried a lot lest he should think I was becoming too dependent on his friendship and on the regularity of our sessions, but clung to the thought that I was giving a little – even if only in the fairly rare boon of having two pianos – as well as taking.

Losing K made me much more passionately 'liberationist' in that it revealed to me very sharply how much greater my resources were than those of a wife who had been totally dependent on her husband, not only financially, but socially. How do they survive, these relicts, these left-over halves of couples who did everything together, whose friends were all couples like themselves, who went everywhere together, had no job but looking after a home and the man who is gone? I had not only ample money and the dignity of a job, but friends of my own – friends whom I had made at work or through my separate interests. They were K's friends too, but initially and permanently *my* friends. They did not slip out of my life when I became a woman on my own. My experience tallied with that of other widows in that my husband's colleagues and men friends fairly quickly drifted out of my life. It caused me some sorrow, but no bitterness. They had their own lives to lead, their own problems. Flaying myself, rather than other widows, I was

144

scornful of women who wail that they are never invited any-where but will not see that they can do the inviting. Cruel, really, because many of us are too broken-backed to make the effort. But the thought served me in my need and drove me to ensure that I was never entirely alone during the long hours of Saturday and Sunday.

It is true what widows say, that our society is cruel to the woman on her own. If we have a party we aim to make our numbers even. A lone woman is a complication. Widows have told me that wives regard them not only as a drag but as a threat – and it seems to be true that some men find the widow irresistibly attractive. My age, no doubt – I was sixty, four years older than K – as well as the sort of company we kept, protected me from passes by men assuming that the widow must be avid for sex, but a curious little experience made me wonder about this apparently quite common approach. I had a very long taxi drive to take across London when ice and snow blocked the traffic and the driver and I began to talk. Soon he was pouring out the whole story of his sex life from the time he was seduced, as a boy, by a much older woman. I arrived at my destination laughing at the thought that someone like me had received these revelations – but wondering whether there may not be some-thing in the body chemistry of the newly bereaved's intensely emotional state that sends out strange signals to the opposite sex. It might help widows in this situation if they could see these sexual approaches as a curious phenomenon rather than a cruel insult. For a great many women, I believe, as for me, grief totally extinguishes sexual desire. But not for all, and the flame may be there, hidden and unacknowledged.

Well, so I planned my days in what I believed to be a very rational, therapeutic way. I gave the go-ahead for the building of a carport K had planned, though the new car had been driven by a friend back to the dealer's within a few days of his death. It would improve the house; it could be let. I agreed with my dear neighbours that they should take over two rooms of our rather curiously interlocked 'semis'. This meant another painful clear out, but it made good sense to reduce the size of my house and increase the size of theirs. I had a flatlet made in my attic and spent long hours clearing out the rubbish – K's way of keep-ing tidy was either to kick rubbish down the cellar steps or cart it up to the attic – then laying lino tiles, staining whitewood furniture, carrying up suitable bits of furniture and equipment. I found a perfect tenant, a young music teacher whom I had met in our choir, whose mixture of independence and friendli-ness was exactly what I needed. I had occasional gatherings of friends. I had a laburnum tree planted in the garden and put in bedding plants and bulbs. I was doing all the kinds of things I urge any widow to do.

And then it hit me. There wasn't any real point in doing any of this. I was hollow inside. I was less than half a person. Behind the carefully maintained façade there was nothing, or at least nothing that really mattered. I must try to explain about this phase of bereavement because only those who have been through it know about it, and it is, I am certain, about three months after the death, when many of us appear to be doing quite nicely, that the collapse of the will to live occurs. It is then that widows, and widowers too, especially if they have no dependent children, need to be taken into the care of their friends. What needs to be done is just to keep them ticking over; to ask them on little visits, give them little jobs to do, nothing very much, nothing very demanding, just small things to fill in the emptiness of the personality as well as of the days. At this stage, Death is the friend, Life is the enemy. It seemed to me at this time that being alive was just a habit, and a habit that had now become very disagreeable. Now I had been jolted out of the normal view that it is obviously better to be alive than dead, it seemed a ludicrous proposition. What was so wonderful about being alive? Sixty years of life had habituated me to eating at certain times, washing, dressing, going to work, doing this and that – but *what for*? Why spend another ten or twenty years doing all these things just for the sake of being alive? There were, it is true, fleeting moments of pleasure but there was nothing, *nothing*, that made the future look anything but a dreary, meaningless trudge. The concept of life as a duty, in the abstract, struck me as monstrous.

Duty to *people*, yes; I had a great, over-riding obligation to my daughter, and could not run away from that. I found the attitude of some spiritualist friends quite baffling. They believed that they were in almost constant touch with loved ones 'on the other side' with whom they would most certainly be re-united after death. Then how, I asked myself, could they bear to wait? What made the idea of speeding the reunion seem so shocking to them?

In fact once my angle of vision on life and death had swung round I believe I got a certain kind of bleak, cynical pleasure from contemplating the view. I was Outside, looking in; un-involved, uncaring, detached; in a sense free. One of my widowed friends told me she threw away her bottle of sleeping pills in case they should be an irresistible temptation. I looked on mine as my greatest comfort and strength, the guarantee that at any time I could quietly decide that enough was enough. Of course that time wasn't to be yet; there was no hope of letting myself off the hook of obligation in the foreseeable future. But *some day* I could lay down my heavy load, say, 'thank you for having me,' and put myself to sleep. I was so much more than 'half in love with easeful death'. Lovely, lovely death; not necessarily an end, not necessarily a beginning. Never once did I allow myself to hope for reunion with K, but I thought that perhaps his 'spirit' if there is such a thing – and mine, one day – might be merged into a sort of stream of consciousness.

Gardening had made me very much aware that in nature nothing ceases to exist. The 'death' of a plant means that it changes its nature, disintegrates into the soil, makes humus, fertilizes other plants. It is hard to believe that what animates a sentient being is lost when the heart ceases to beat; the beating of the heart, the inflation of the lungs are an explanation of how life is maintained, not in any sense an explanation of what life *is*. What was the impulse that *made* the heart beat, the lungs inflate, I kept asking myself; what was the impulse that enabled the brain cells to collate and transform the information transmitted to them by the senses of Beethoven's *Eroica* or Shakespeare's *Hamlet*? Why should this impulse, analogous, I thought, to electro-magnetic waves, stop short when the heart stopped beating? The unplugging of a television set does not mean that the electro-magnetic waves cease to flow, only that they cease to function at that particular point of outlet.

What drove me to explore these ideas was the sense that K's death had not only bereaved but mutilated me. Whatever he was and whatever I was had become so inextricably mingled through thirty years together that when what was K was abruptly wrenched away the machine for living that was Mary seemed to be lacking some essential parts. When two integrated psyches are severed there *must* be damage. I thought then that the damage to mine was permanent and I am sure that with some people it is so. My psyche proved to be stronger than I thought – indeed, than I hoped, for at this stage I bitterly resented the idea that I should be clutched back into the habit of living, that the instinctive will to live might reassert itself and that in old age I might lose the will to die, which to me would be a very shameful thing.

The time stretched out. There was the job, which in 1968 took a challenging new shape, the family, music, the house and garden, friends. Helen invited me to join her and another friend on a crazy car trip through Rumania and Hungary. I, a non-driver, often sat broodily for long hours in the back of the car, wedged between sleeping bags and luggage but we shared much hilarity in our search for overnight accommodation. Perhaps the discovery that mourning does not preclude bellyaching

147

laughter is a turning point. It takes a long while for the bereaved to experience conscious happiness; much longer to admit to being happy, for that seems an intolerable disloyalty. Yet the return to normality has to be at the cost of the recession of the lost one. One may say, and often does, that the bloodiest anguish is better than forgetting, but the anguish slowly, and by no means steadily, recedes too. When K broke a leg it took him many months to acquire confidence in putting his weight on it again, but the day did come when he realized that for days, or for weeks, he had been walking quite naturally. That is how it is with the crippling effect of grief. Life creeps in unawares to restore the mutilated personality. For weeks I was a non-person; for many, many months a half person and now I have to admit – reluctantly, because it was better to be part of a dual entity – that I am at least as much a whole person as many people who have never been chopped in half. I never consciously sought to create 'a life of my own', nor indeed actively hoped for or wanted it. It just happened, gradually, by doing what I had to do, by very determinedly filling up all the hours so that I seldom mouldered away on my own, by responding civilly, even if not with enthusiasm, to whatever invitations or stimuli came my way – and by quite savagely rejecting the idea that the widow should be a lifelong object of pity or, indeed, is more to be pitied than many other people who have suffered cruel loss or rejection, or who have never enjoyed the fullness of life. Several times I explored this thought in my *Guardian* writings and once with a hard irony that, to my sorrow, caused acute pain to women whose bereavement, whose wounds, were more raw than mine. It was about The Club, that sisterhood for widows which can be such a tender support and such a dangerous encouragement to trying to live in the past. Should I have written it, should it have been published? I don't know. I only know that if the mutilated personality is to survive it cannot be by trying to keep the Other alive, by emotional self-indulgence; it can only be by letting the habit of living take over until one can respond again to what life has to offer. As it gradually took over for me.

I had one more hurdle to surmount. The house; the garden. In the summer of 1969 Helen and I spent a month in America, crossing the continent together by Greyhound bus to Los Angeles, then separating and meeting up in New York for the return journey. I had friends in Los Angeles, San Francisco, Washington, New York. Not all the intervening bits were easy, though I managed a solitary birthday in an isolated motel in Trinidad, North California, pretty well. I got home very early on a beautiful, sunny July morning to find a notice on the door,

148

Welcome to Home Sweet Home. We're all here' – perhaps the sweetest, most heart-warming thing my daughter ever did for me, and I drifted round the garden cutting off the dead rose heads, very much in love with its healing beauty, until it seemed time to make a pot of tea for us all. But from that time the thought began to take shape, 'What am I doing, maintaining this large house, this very large garden, just for me?' (Fortunately my dear tenant was at the same time beginning to feel the need for a house of her own.)

That I could begin, very gingerly at first, to explore the idea of moving was an indication of how far I had moved, in less than two years, along the road to being a separate entity again, for it was probably in our attachment to this house and garden that we had been most closely integrated. We had lived there nearly twenty years. If I went, I left most of my life with K behind – for to move to a smaller home in Manchester, where all our married life had been spent, made no sense at all. My only child lived in London and I was within sight of retirement, when I could need contact with her and her family more than ever. If I stayed, I had evidences of K's presence all about me – but they must have been fading a little, or how could I have even begun to think of pulling up the roots that spread so deep and wide? So it is for many of us – within two years we become able to act rationally, no longer instinctively. Reason said 'Go', and having established with the editor of the *Guardian* that my move to the London office would not be unwelcome, I set about the next bloody, brutal surgical operation, by putting the house up for sale. I am glad now, though I was very disconcerted then, that a firm offer for it came within days, for it forced me into action – into finding a flat in Blackheath, reasonably near to my daughter, and into going again through all the goods we had accumulated together, and into discarding what could not be fitted into three rooms, boxroom, kitchen and bathroom. Of course it was sickeningly painful. How could it be otherwise? Yet working out with pencil, paper, ruler, measuring tape, which carpets, which furniture would fit where and hold what, was an interesting and therapeutic exercise. All intellectual exercises are therapeutic once the wits have begun to function again.

So in February, 1970 I came to London and after the inevitably miserable, frustrating, lonely weeks of settling into the flat, what I had thought to be a decaying plant's feeble suckers proved to be viable new growth. A person began to emerge who might not have been able, or wished, to emerge had our joint life continued. K would have been very happy that the expansion of the *Guardian*'s influence and success meant a small

149

expansion of my own success and that opportunities came my way which might not have arisen in Manchester. It was not in his nature to be envious of any success of mine. Indeed, why should he be? He had a reputation in his own field as a newspaper executive which survives him. Men still come up to me and say affectionately, 'He was a man's man,' meaning he was a leader of men. But how would he have liked my involvement with the sisters of Women's Liberation? Not much, especially the thought of my carrying a banner, risking conflict with the police! And I was very willing to play the role of Caesar's wife, and am not embarrassed to say so. I owed my partner so much that it was no conscious sacrifice to refrain from any action, any writing, that would even fractionally embarrass, hurt or damage him. But now I am alone I am free. Sometimes I am very lonely, and more painfully so when there is some small triumph or success and no one to rejoice with me, than in trouble or disappointment. But freedom has its compensations – freedom to come and go; freedom to do the things one refrained from doing before; freedom to explore new patterns of life; freedom, if one has a mind to it, to become an elderly eccentric.

Elderly. That is a thought I should take into my mind now I am in my mid-sixties and retired from full-time work. Elderly. How absurd. I no longer run for buses or upstairs, but I chase small Charlotte round the garden or up and down the corridor. I dance with her and carry her around. I exchange clothes, including velvet trouser suits, with my elegant daughter. I sit in the bar of the Press Club with my women friends. I dig in the garden without puffing or creaking. I am off to Israel, Scotland, the Isle of Wight, on a painting holiday to Spain. Soon I shall have more time for duets. I lost the habit of sitting down and relaxing with TV or knitting or gramophone records when K died and Radio is always the friend in the house. I am not deceiving myself about the quality of my life. It is quite rich, quite enviable. I do not need to wonder yet, I think, how long I have left to enjoy the mental and physical pleasures of being alive.

Shall I put away then for a while the thought that the body will inevitably deteriorate and the mind with it? I think I safely can, for I still feel no shrinking from the thought of death. Alex Comfort, reviewing Simone de Beauvoir's *Old Age* in March 1972, wrote of death, to my surprise and dismay, as 'an irreconcilable enemy' to which the 'natural reaction is outrage and resentment'; as 'the final dissolution, as Gerontius said, "of all that makes me Man" '. But I think that death may not be the final dissolution, and that it is not the quenching of the tiny spark of 'life' that animates the body that is outrageous but that the dissolution should be slow, humiliating, poverty-stricken, lonely. So let the politicians concern themselves that old age should not be feared because of poverty, as it was feared when it meant the workhouse; let the doctors concern themselves with removing the fear of progressive diseases which slowly paralyse the mental and physical faculties, and not with frantic efforts to fan that little spark in a hopelessly malfunctioning body. And let not the gerontologists bemuse us with the thought that the span of life must be stretched further and further and further because it is obviously better to be alive than dead. There are far too many old people cluttering up the earth now and if we were not so afraid of death we should be able to see that to deny life to the unborn while determinedly prolonging the life of the worn-out old is a very strange illogicality.

Why are we so afraid to be dead? We are no longer afraid of hellfire. Is it that we have been deprived of the hope of heaven? Isn't sweet oblivion enough? Perhaps one day physicists exploring the ultimate constituents of the universe, energy and mass, particle and wave, and the parapsychologists exploring the strange phenomena of thought and 'mind' – which are only inexplicable, they might say, because we don't know enough and have, since the age of nineteenth-century materialism, been living in 'the country of the blind' – may join together to provide us with a substitute for heaven, some meaning and purpose in Life beyond what we can now grasp while we totter around on our two uncertain legs in the space–time continuum. Something to look forward to?

As for me, it is because death is still the friend that life has ceased to be the enemy. Whatever happens, hopefully when *I* choose, there will be an end. And perhaps a beginning.